A road map for achieving your goals and surviving success.

Spell SUCCESS in your Life

Peter Colwell

Manjul Publishing House Pvt. Ltd.

DISCLAIMER

This book is designed to provide practical ways to live a better life. It in no way serves as a substitute for professional counseling or therapy. Every effort has been made by the author, editor, and publisher to produce a complete and accurate book.

The purpose of this book is to motivate and inspire. The author and Manjul Publishing House shall have neither liability nor responsibility to any person or entity with respect to any loss or damage caused, or alleged to have been caused, directly or indirectly, by the information contained in this book.

Spell SUCCESS in Your Life
A Road Map for Achieving Your Goals
and Surviving Success
by Peter G Colwell

First published in India by

Manjul Publishing House Pvt. Ltd.
10, Nishat Colony, 74 Bungalows, Bhopal, India 462 003
Ph. : +91 755 5240340 Fax : +91 755 2736919
E-mail : manjulindia@sancharnet.in

First published - 2003

ISBN - 81 - 86775 - 36 - 6

Printed in India by
Thomson Press (India) Ltd., New Delhi, INDIA

Dedication

To Trevia-Lynne,
who paints a picture of love in my heart every day.

Thank you for your love and inspiration
throughout the entire creation of this book.

I love you today, tomorrow, and forever!

In Loving Memory of
Christian Victoria "Chrissie" Carrigan
(November 14, 1986 – December 6, 2001)

*"You were an earthly angel called home too soon.
We love you, angel butterfly!"*

What People Are Saying About "Spell SUCCESS in Your Life"

"I love this book! Pure motivation from start to finish! With Peter's guidance, and your own hunger to succeed, you can shake off mediocrity and become the person you've always wanted to be."

LES BROWN
Author
Live Your Dreams and
It's Not Over Until You Win!

"*Spell SUCCESS in Your Life* speaks to the heart and soul. In this book, Peter Colwell shows you that your success never has to reach a dead end. Read it and re-read it, and learn to truly enjoy the success journey."

WILLIE JOLLEY
Author
It Only Takes a Minute to Change Your Life! and *A Setback Is a Setup for a Comeback*

"Become a success insider by reading and applying the insights contained herein."

MARK VICTOR HANSEN
Co-creator
#1 *New York Times* best-selling series *Chicken Soup for the Soul®*

"The only success that matters is balanced, dealing with your whole life. This book gives you a blueprint to make your life a masterpiece!"

BRIAN TRACY
Author
The 100 Absolutely Unbreakable Laws of Business Success

"This is one of the most practical books on success I have read. Peter Colwell offers steps anyone can take to live a life not only of success, but also of significance."

CRAIG VALENTINE, MBA
1999 World Champion of Public Speaking

"A must book for success! The truly successful person must have perspective, preparation, and patience. Peter Colwell shows us the way. The true key to success is conditioning. If we apply Peter's unique interactive techniques, we will condition ourselves for true success in whatever goals we set for ourselves."

BENNIE BOUGH
Past President
Toastmasters International

"*Spell SUCCESS in Your Life* is a must-read guide for anyone who desires a successful life and needs the coaching and direction to get there. Peter does a fantastic job of instructing and preparing you for the true greatness that you are destined for. You will find this book hard to put down."

DEWAYNE OWENS
Author
How to Get Rich on PURPOSE

"Spirited, clear, and motivating! What makes Peter's book so special? He dares to practice what he preaches. A lot of people write and talk about achieving their goals. Peter Colwell lives it."

MICHELLE JAMES
President
Creations Unlimited

"For those struggling and striving for greatness, Peter Colwell lays out an inspirational blueprint in his skillfully written *Spell SUCCESS in Your Life*. The highly readable chapters are insightful, understandable, and packed with practical how-to steps for professional and personal success. Colwell's battle-tested formulas draw on his personal anecdotes as well as the wisdom of the ages. Brimming with enthusiasm, Colwell becomes a personal life coach who helps the reader develop lifetime habits for achievement. An excellent resource – relevant and real – that you'll want to keep handy to stoke those motivational fires again and again."

MELISSA CHARBONNEAU
White House Correspondent
CBN News

"True leaders walk their talk! Peter Colwell walks his talk BIG TIME in this motivational, uplifting book! Buy a copy for yourself and a few extras for your family and friends who need inspiration to make their dreams come true. They will thank you for it!"

BARBARA BROWN
President, Leader Learning
Professional Speaker,
Seminar Leader, and Trainer

"This book is so inspirational and informative, and most of all it has a very sensible approach. If you follow this step-by-step approach, you will have to attain some level of success, even in spite of yourself, depending on the effort you put into it. You will be surprised at what you can accomplish, and you'll find yourself on a positive road to even more fulfillment of your dreams."

DOTTI PIANO
Team Leader
Dale Carnegie Course in Effective Speaking
and Human Relations

Acknowledgments

I would like to thank all of my friends and family who believed that my dream of becoming a published author was more than just a dream!

Special thanks go to my mom and dad, Marjorie and Peter Colwell, who brought me into this world twenty-seven years ago! Thank you for your encouraging ears from the very first paragraph four years ago to the final touches on the closing sentence.

To Susan, my older sister and closest friend, for all of your love and support throughout my life.

To Chris Johnson, my best friend and confidante. Thanks for your rock-solid friendship over the years, and for always reminding me to "think big."

To "Mom" and "Dad" Carrigan, for knowing all along that I could do it — and reminding me!

To my editor and friend, Peter Vogt, first of all, for "getting" the book concept without any explanation needed whatsoever, for your thoughtful, guiding hand and sense of humor throughout the entire editing process, and for actually making it an enjoyable experience! Who knew editing could be so much fun?

To two of the sweetest and most professional people I've ever worked with — Tami Dever and Erin Stark of TLC Graphics — for making my life so much easier than it could have been, and for having unlimited enthusiasm about my book from the moment we met. You knew exactly what I was looking for, and exceeded my expectations for the design and layout of this book.

To Bonnie Maidak, for being "on call" to proofread the final, typeset manuscript. Thank you for providing valuable, last-minute insights to help ensure complete accuracy.

To my friend and mentor, Larry Welch, for your encouragement, support, and kindness, inside and outside of Toastmasters.

Many thanks to Les Brown, for honoring me with a Foreword and believing in my book way before anybody knew about it.

Thanks to Michelle James for taking an interest in my book from the get-go, and for being the first to get my ideas published. Thank you for your creative feedback on the first drafts and your unique insights on success.

To my former literary agent, Douglas Storey, for taking an interest in my project in the early stages.

Special thanks to the following individuals for the gift of your time, talent, and interest in helping support my book project: Barbara Brown, Shelly Williams, Mike and Linda Schultz, William Moore, Ada Bowlding, Mark Anderson, Willie Jolley, Craig Valentine, Dotti Piano, Melissa Charbonneau, Ken Lane, Diane Beliveau, DeWayne Owens, Bennie Bough, Kate Kennedy, Jean Asher, Pam Bankett, David Larsen, Elizabeth Tsai, Deborah Hall, Barbara Casey, Linda Putz, Trudy Marschall, Tom Corbley, and John Wallace.

To Dan Poynter, Bobbie Christensen, Marilyn and Tom Ross, and Dottie Walters, for shortening my learning curve as a publisher and speaker.

Finally, to my wife, Trevia-Lynne — my rock — for reminding me when things got tough to keep on writing because "you have a message that people need to read." Glad I listened to you! Your love and support have made this book possible. I love you always!

Foreword

It isn't every day that a book comes along and changes your life. Many books entertain and educate their readers. Some even go as far as to leave a favorable, lasting impression. ***Spell SUCCESS in Your Life*** will help you develop a game plan for achieving your goals, and will inspire you to turn your most treasured dreams into rock-solid reality.

In this book, Peter Colwell outlines specific steps you can take to move from the thinking phase to the action phase with respect to your dreams and aspirations. Peter teaches you that to create positive, meaningful change in your life, you need to believe in yourself and take action on your goals. I often tell people in my seminars that history is replete with folks who took their dreams and ideas with them to their graves. This book is a stark reminder of everyone's need to avoid the very costly mistake of letting life "live you."

This book will motivate you to look past your limitations and to eliminate negative forces in your life that sidetrack you from your destination. With Peter's guidance, and your own hunger to succeed, you can shake off mediocrity and become the person you've always wanted to be! I encourage you to read this book and apply these simple principles in your life to achieve the recognition and success you deserve.

Unlike other books on self-improvement, ***Spell SUCCESS in Your Life*** tells you how to cope with the newfound attention and praise that often accompany success, and how to perpetuate the process of achievement over and over again throughout your personal and professional adventures.

To truly live your dreams, you must be willing to do whatever it takes to change your life. This book will be a stepping-stone on your way!

Les Brown
Author
Live Your Dreams
It's Not Over Until You Win!

Table of Contents

Introduction

How do you spell "success"? Is it a life of luxury and wealth? Earning a Ph.D. in your chosen field? Running a marathon or perhaps conquering your first mile? Certainly "success" means different things to different people. Contentment is attainable to both the rich and the poor. Satisfaction is within reach for those who are single as well as those who are in relationships. Many paths lead to success and fulfillment in life.

The purpose of *Spell SUCCESS in Your Life* is to give you a practical, creative guide to successful living. When we are born, nobody hands us an *Instructional Guide to Life 101*. We don't receive uniform rules on how to live our lives effectively, on what path we should follow, or what beliefs we should adopt. Instead, we must find our own way through the winding trails and valleys of life.

Even those who are fortunate enough to be blessed with loving guidance from parents, friends, teachers, and others need to find their own path — the path that will lead to inner peace and happiness. So using the seven letters in the word S-U-C-C-E-S-S, I've developed a road map you can use to guide yourself throughout life in any endeavor:

Strive

Understand

Create

Condition

Envision

Savor

Soar

You can use this conceptualization to navigate any area of your life — personal goals, career objectives, financial dreams, physical development, or spiritual awareness. Regardless of what your idea of "success" may be, where you're "at" in your life, or what your specific goals and dreams are, this road map has universal applications for you. Apply it to your own life and circumstances and you'll achieve the results you desire.

By employing the techniques and principles in this book in your daily life, you'll develop a **belief** in yourself, a **passion** for living, the **perseverance** to help you reach and even exceed your goals, and the **enthusiasm** you need to follow through with your plans — whether you are a:

- High school or college student preparing for the "real world."
- Career changer searching for a new, more fulfilling work path.
- Longtime employee who's thinking of becoming an entrepreneur.
- Committed self-improver who's ready to make some positive changes.
- Success-minded person preparing to take your personal and professional achievement to the next level.

We all need something to hold on to — something to solidify or validate our beliefs. Since creating this SUCCESS formula, I've actively used it in my own life and have seen incredible results. I've trained for and completed two marathons, something I'd always considered impossible. I've met and married the woman of my dreams. And I've gotten involved with Toastmasters International, a group that has helped me develop myself as a speaker and leader, and learn how to express myself more creatively and effectively.

Let me briefly illustrate how I used my SUCCESS formula to achieve one particular goal: Training for and completing my first marathon. The first step I took was to **Strive** — to set a goal for myself. My goal was to train for and successfully complete a 26.2-mile race. So I first wrote my goal down. Then, I became excited about the prospect of achieving the ultimate physical and mental challenge, and started telling people about my goal without worrying about what they might think.

Next, I set out to **Understand** what reaching my goal would require of me. I asked myself questions like:

- What do I need to do?
- What skills do I need to develop?
- What action(s) do I need to take to reach my goal?

I soon realized that I needed to start an exercise program to increase my cardiovascular fitness. I also needed to develop a plan for how many times per week I would work out. And I needed to figure out what types of aerobic training I would do.

Then, I decided to take action and get started. I threw aside excuses for not following through — such as the fact that I'd never run more than a mile in my life, or that I was potentially being unrealistic — and just did it: I decided to **Create** the conditions that would ultimately lead to my success, the key word there being "**ultimately**." I bought some running shoes and started running, with visions of *Forrest Gump* in my mind: "I ran and I ran and I ran … and I just kept running." I determined my level of fitness and worked to improve it just a little bit each week, measuring my progress along the way by keeping a log of my workouts.

The next step was one of the most critical to achieving my goal: I was determined to **Condition** myself mentally, emotionally, and physically to reach my goal. I read books on marathon training and conditioning. I received advice from trainers and runners alike. I told myself that finishing a marathon was not only possible for me, but that it would actually happen. I learned to believe in myself and my goal — and I poured my whole self into reaching that goal!

Throughout my training and conditioning, I continually visualized myself running the whole course, full of stamina and endurance. I pictured the crowd cheering me on. I saw my family members bursting with pride on the sidelines, waving balloons and yelling my name with joy and enthusiasm. During practice runs, I would wave to the trees and the river on each side of me, imagining that they were crowds of supporters urging me along the way. I would **Envision** myself approaching the last leg of the race, nearing the final few yards. I'd see myself gaining momentum and sprinting to the finish line!

Finally, the day of the marathon arrived — the moment I had long anticipated and envisioned. I wanted to **Savor** every moment of this day, from my early-morning wake-up, to my pre-race stretching, to the starting gun, to each of the 26.2 miles and the final steps to the finish line. Why was this experience so important to me? Here's an excerpt from my personal training log, written soon after the marathon:

All that hard work and dedication paid off. I learned so much about myself and my inner strength and determination. When I commit myself to a task, there is **nothing** that will stand in my way of achieving it! I felt like a little kid all over again. I was so excited as the day approached — two more weeks … one more week … three more days … 48 hours left! The build-up was incredible! I've never been so excited about anything in my whole life!

As you can see, I made the most of every moment, knowing that each of them passes quickly. In the process, I enriched the experience itself.

The final step on the way to my goal was to **Soar**. After basking in my accomplishment, feeling like king for a day, I resolved to set new goals for myself. I have since run another marathon, and I plan to keep running and improving my level of fitness.

I recommend this SUCCESS formula to you and to anyone else who wants to achieve his or her goals and dreams. Throughout my personal development, the "7 Letters of SUCCESS" concept has served as a model for helping me reach my goals and better understand myself. It's a concept that consistently inspires me — and I'd like it to inspire you, too.

I hope you'll reap tremendous value from *Spell SUCCESS in Your Life*, and that you'll use the book's ideas to create for yourself a life that is richer, happier, and more fulfilling.

Peter Colwell
Germantown, Maryland
February 2002

ONE

STRIVE

Pour your Soul Into your Goal

"Success is the ongoing process of striving to become more."

— ANTHONY ROBBINS

It has often been said that the joy of living lies in working toward something: A personal or professional goal, or perhaps a new way of thinking or behaving. In fact, I would go so far as to say that we spend the majority of our lives reaching and stretching in the direction of our various pursuits. All of our time, thoughts, and energies are devoted to the attainment of these ends. Certainly, **Striving** is one important element of being successful.

We should be striving for something every day, whether it be to improve our job performance, lose those few extra pounds, devote more attention to our loved ones, or pay off our seemingly endless financial debts. When we have goals to strive for, our lives take on new meaning. We gain vitality and a sense of purpose. Life becomes exciting!

CHOOSE THE RIGHT GOALS

What goals are right for you? Which ones are really worth pursuing — worth striving for? Personal goals should be **challenging** and **worthwhile**. You need goals that will excite you, drive you, even inspire you! Make sure the goals you choose will benefit you in some way, and that they're consistent with your values. Otherwise you probably won't follow through on them. Goals are worthwhile because of the ultimate benefits you envision deriving from them. If you can clearly picture the eventual fruits of your labor, you'll have a great source of motivation en route to your dreams.

One effective method for setting goals is to make a list featuring your **goals** in one column and the **benefits** you expect to receive from achieving those goals in another column. This method works best when you write down your most important goals for the coming months. These must be goals that mean a lot to you — powerful goals that put a smile on your face each day and make you bounce out of bed in anticipation and excitement! I call these types of goals *power goals*; the benefits you'll receive from achieving them are thus *power benefits*.

Make a list of your five most important goals for the coming year and why they're so important to you. (Note: If necessary, use a separate piece of paper so that you have plenty of room to write. You might even want to buy a small notebook that you can use to complete all of the exercises in this book.) Be specific:

POWER GOALS	*POWER BENEFITS*
1. ____________________	1. ____________________
2. ____________________	2. ____________________
3. ____________________	3. ____________________
4. ____________________	4. ____________________
5. ____________________	5. ____________________

SEEK BALANCE IN YOUR GOALS

Life is one great balancing act, no question about it. Therefore, we must always strive for moderation and a sense of balance in our duties and responsibilities, as well as in our goals. Let's face it: There are **many** areas of our lives that we can improve. The difficult part is fulfilling certain needs without neglecting other important needs — in other words, finding a **balance**.

In order to pursue fulfillment in all areas of our lives, we need to have goals for each area. So set a few primary goals in each of the following categories:

- Personal
- Career
- Financial
- Physical
- Spiritual
- Family
- Community
- Other

You may find that one or two of these categories deserve extra emphasis. If so, pay particular attention to these areas of your life. Often, for example, people sacrifice their personal or family lives in pursuit of their careers. As a result, their marriages and intimate relationships suffer. Or, conversely, some people trade their careers for their personal and family lives: They settle down and build a family while burying their dreams. In still other situations, people let themselves go physically in order to enjoy personal pleasures. So it's important to try to strike a balance with your goals.

List two or three goals for each area of your life. Remember to be specific:

PERSONAL

____

____

____

CAREER

____

____

____

FINANCIAL

____

____

____

PHYSICAL

SPIRITUAL

FAMILY

COMMUNITY

OTHER

Now, determine when you'd like to achieve each of these goals. Again, be specific and give yourself a deadline. (Remember: A goal isn't a goal unless it's specific and has a definite timetable.) Try to be reasonable yet ambitious:

PERSONAL

CAREER

FINANCIAL

PHYSICAL

SPIRITUAL

FAMILY

____

____

____

COMMUNITY

____

____

____

OTHER

____

____

____

Finally, think about and write down the reasons these goals are worthwhile for you. Ask yourself, "How will achieving these goals improve my life and benefit me?" If you focus on the ultimate benefits you'll receive and picture how achieving these goals will make you feel, you'll greatly increase your chances of succeeding.

Five Ways to Find a Healthy Balance Among Your Goals

It's easy to make a list of goals you would like to achieve. It's a lot more difficult to follow through with them when distractions, fatigue, stress, and confusion get in the way. The following techniques will help you reduce stress and make time for your most important goals:

Say "No" More Than You Say "Yes"

Often, it seems like we're programmed to please other people and to place their priorities ahead of our own. Does this sound like something you typically find yourself doing? When we consistently put other people's needs ahead of our own, our lives get out of sync. We become overwhelmed with the little details, fatigued at the end of the day, and prone to a multitude of potentially harmful health problems. You can solve this problem by learning to say "no" more often than you say "yes" to obligations and commitments.

For example, when someone asks for your help on a project you know you don't have time for, say, "I'd love to help out on the project, but I have to say 'no' this time. Keep me in mind next time." (Say that only if you mean it, of course!) If your schedule is booked solid, you can politely turn down a speaking invitation by replying, "I'm honored that you've invited me to speak to your group next week. However, my schedule won't permit me to make it. Thanks for the generous offer, though!" By showing sincere appreciation when you turn down someone's request or offer, you'll smooth over an otherwise awkward situation.

Declining people's requests may be uncomfortable at first; but after a while, you'll appreciate the extra time and energy you can devote to your own needs.

Clear Your Calendar

Every once in a while, it's a good idea to erase everything on your calendar for a few days (unless you have a critical doctor's appointment or your kid's soccer game!). Instead, pencil in time for you to meditate, go for an afternoon jog, or take in a movie at your local cinema. Then add the other items to your calendar — but without filling it up completely. Do this as often as necessary, especially when you are feeling overwhelmed with your day-to-day schedule.

Reflect on What's Missing in Your Life

The fast pace of everyday life can swallow your passion for living and drain you of the very energy you need to pursue your goals. In *Take Time for Your Life* (Broadway Books, 1999), professional speaker and life coach Cheryl Richardson encourages us to make self-care our No. 1 priority. She advises us to slow down from the frenetic pace of daily life and determine what essential ingredients are missing in our lives. Maybe you need to focus more on your spirituality. Maybe your physical well-being needs to become a top priority. Take the time to assess your physical, emotional, and spiritual needs, whatever they may be.

Get a TPO — a Third-Party Opinion

Sometimes we're too close to our own work and daily patterns to realize that things have gotten out of control. It's only when your best friend reaches you at the office at 9 p.m. that you awaken to the fact that maybe you're putting in too many hours at the office. Or maybe you haven't had a decent night's sleep in months, and you find yourself nodding off at the wheel on the interstate highway. These are just a couple of the many instances in which you should ask for a TPO — a Third-Party Opinion — from someone who cares enough about you to tell it like it is. You'll thank the person for it!

Get off the "Ladder"

Dr. Stephen Covey, best-selling author of *The 7 Habits of Highly Effective People* (Simon & Schuster, 1990), uses a powerful metaphor to illustrate the uncertainty and surprise many people face when they realize they've spent months, if not years, climbing up the corporate or professional "ladder," only to realize one day that their "ladder" has been leaning against the wrong wall! What they assumed would be a "pot of gold at the end of the rainbow" — such as a corner office or a cushy executive job — ends up instead being a life of emptiness and frustration. Many businesspeople refer to this phenomenon as the "golden handcuffs syndrome." At any point in your climb toward success, you may want to follow in the footsteps of thousands of wise people who simply got off the ladder and followed their **true** passions.

Using these five strategies, work to strike a balance among your goals — so that you don't shortchange yourself in the pursuit of what you consider to be "success."

STRETCH YOUR IMAGINATION

Setting creative and fulfilling goals requires you to stretch your imagination about what's possible to achieve. To find the right mix of daring, challenging, and fun goals, consider what you'd like to accomplish over the span of your lifetime, what qualities you'd like to develop to reach those goals, and what skills you need to acquire to maximize your chances of living your dream life:

LIST 10 THINGS YOU'D LIKE TO ACCOMPLISH IN YOUR LIFETIME:

____

____

____

____

____

____

____

____

____

____

LIST FIVE QUALITIES YOU'D LIKE TO "OVERHEAR" OTHER PEOPLE ATTRIBUTE TO YOU:

____

____

____

____

____

LIST ONE THING THAT'S HOLDING YOU BACK FROM SETTING OUT TO ACHIEVE MANY, IF NOT ALL, OF THESE GOALS:

____

WHAT ARE YOU GOOD AT THAT YOU COULD BECOME BETTER AT?

____

____

____

ARE YOU WILLING TO:

- Devote more time to your goals?
- Get up early or stay up late, if necessary, to achieve your goals?
- Miss out on social opportunities in order to achieve your goals?
- Invest a significant amount of energy and attention in your goals?

WHAT ARE YOU WILLING TO GIVE UP IN PURSUIT OF YOUR GOALS?

____

____

____

WHAT WILL YOU ABSOLUTELY NOT GIVE UP IN PURSUIT OF YOUR GOALS?

____

____

____

____

____

____

CAN YOU FIND A "HAPPY COMPROMISE" BETWEEN EACH GOAL AND YOUR VALUES? IF NOT, ARE YOU WILLING TO FORSAKE CERTAIN GOALS FOR OTHERS?

____

MAKE YOURSELF ACCOUNTABLE

One important thing to remember as you make your way up the ladder of success is that **whether you succeed or fail depends entirely upon one person: you**! When you hold yourself accountable for your attitude and your actions — by acknowledging that your past thoughts and decisions have led you to your present circumstances — you're able to take charge of your outcomes by giving yourself the chance to make better decisions in the future. *Accountability* is the notion of accepting responsibility for what your life looks like now. "Making yourself accountable" helps you deal with the present challenges in your life and move past them.

In what areas of your life do you need to "make yourself accountable"? Here are some possibilities:

- Your punctuality (or lack thereof).
- Your smoking habit.
- Your tendency to overeat.
- Your frequent use of bad language.
- Your ability (or lack thereof) to follow through on your promises.
- Your commitment (or lack thereof) to physical fitness.

- Your willingness to spend quality time with your significant other.
- Your ability to balance work with the rest of your life.

Commit yourself to becoming the person you want to be by making yourself accountable in an area of your life that needs improvement. You might, for example, hold yourself accountable for being on time for work, interviews, appointments, or meetings with friends. As you become more responsible, other people will respect and appreciate you more.

Here are three other specific benefits of taking complete responsibility for your life:

- **You increase your self-confidence** — When you take full responsibility for your life, suddenly there's no one else to blame. If you're overweight and you decide to become accountable for your obesity (unless you have a thyroid condition or unusually low metabolism due to a pre-existing medical condition), you can no longer blame those tempting commercials and magazine ads for your problem. You can no longer make excuses like "I don't have time to get to the gym" or "My friends always give me their leftovers." Once you make a commitment to stopping the pattern of your self-destructive behavior, your confidence will grow. You'll have more control over your life — and it will feel good!
- **You give yourself a renewed sense of purpose** — Once you commit to being accountable in a specific area of your life, you'll feel empowered to follow through with that commitment. To make sure your motivation doesn't fade away or falter, remind yourself daily about why this commitment is important to you and how you'll benefit from it — how your life will be changed for the better. Honest and periodic assessments will allow you to determine how close you are to fulfilling your commitment, what else you need to do to actually fulfill it, and what changes you may need to make to get it all just right.
- **You become the navigator in your own journey** — Make sure the journey you're traveling is your own. Ask yourself, "Am I living according to my own expectations or the expectations of others?" Many people get caught in the trap of living someone else's dream instead of their own. If you want to make great strides toward improving your life, you must hold yourself to your *own* high standards. Parents, teachers, and coaches can offer you guidance and structure, but ultimately you must hold yourself accountable for your actions. This doesn't mean you need to be a perfectionist, or that you should

beat yourself up over mistakes and setbacks. Changing your attitudes and behaviors is a gradual process of ups and downs. So give yourself permission to mess up once in a while. Failed attempts usually build character anyway — because they allow you to learn from what went wrong and find ways to do things differently next time.

DEVELOP A SENSE OF MISSION

One way to stay focused on your goals is to follow in the footsteps of many organizations, companies, and even individuals: Create a ***mission statement*** that describes what you'd like to achieve in your life, what legacy you'd like to leave to your family and to society, and, perhaps most importantly, what kind of person you'd like to become.

Maybe you want to spend more time with your loved ones and make family a priority in your life. Maybe you'd like to be more empathetic and become a better listener. Whatever you'd like to do, write it down. Then look at your "mission statement" once or twice a day, until it permeates your subconscious mind and becomes second nature to you.

Your mission statement can range in length from a sentence or two to a few bullet points or a few paragraphs. Brevity is usually best, however, since it helps you remember the main point(s) of your statement and increases the chances that you'll actually carry out your mission.

Here is my personal mission statement:

Mission Statement of Peter Colwell

I, Peter Glenn Colwell, hereby commit myself to achieving and living up to the following standards, as long as I live:

- To develop a deep level of self-awareness.
- To set exciting and challenging goals for myself.
- To live life with a sense of urgency.
- To seek and acknowledge greatness in others.
- To never settle for less than I can become or accomplish.
- To serve God, my family, my friends, and my community.
- To awaken myself to different cultures, belief systems, and customs.
- To remain true to myself, my values, and my ideals.
- To avoid compromising my integrity.
- To live my dreams.

- To try to see the larger picture.
- To constantly "raise the bar" and find ways to improve myself.
- To become an inspirational leader of the 21st century.
- To become an awe-inspiring motivational speaker.
- To never lose sight of my most treasured values: love, friendship, loyalty, family, and faith.
- To appreciate my God-given talents and abilities.
- To contribute to improving the quality of people's lives.

With your mission statement in place, you'll develop a "can do" mentality: There will be no more "ifs," "ands," "buts," or "maybes" where your goals are concerned.

The beauty of creating a mission statement is that you give yourself something to live up to. The only person you have to answer to is **yourself!** By developing a mission statement, you hold **yourself** accountable for your life.

What's your mission all about? What are your long-term goals? What kind of person do you want to become? What attributes must you develop to help you achieve your goals? Ask yourself the following questions:

WHAT DO I WANT TO DO WITH MY LIFE?

____

____

____

WHO DO I WANT TO BECOME IN THE PROCESS?

____

____

____

WHERE DO I WANT TO GO?

____

____

____

WHEN DO I WANT TO GET THERE?

____

____

____

WHY WILL IT BENEFIT ME?

____

____

____

HOW WILL I MAKE IT HAPPEN?

____

____

____

TAKE A "SIP" OF SUCCESS

Before we can truly "taste" success — the kind that is lasting and real — we need to build a foundation of *Self-esteem, Integrity,* and *Priorities.*

What happens when your self-esteem is eroded? Your relationships flounder. You lack the commitment and follow-through you need to deliver on your promises. You become disillusioned with your life.

What happens when you take shortcuts and look for the "easy way out" of situations? Typically, looking for the "quick fix" or the "one-size-fits-all" solution only leads to failure and embarrassment instead.

What happens when you place too much importance on your career and you forget about your family and other loved ones? You wind up with an imbalance in your priorities that leads to broken families, stale relationships, and internal feelings of "emptiness."

When you feel good about yourself, on the other hand — and when you focus on what's really important to you — you'll begin to truly "SIP" success:

S*elf-esteem* — A Precious Gift

I*ntegrity* — Go for the "Gold"!

P*riorities* — Know Your Bottom Line

Self-Esteem: A Precious Gift

I cannot overemphasize the importance of *self-esteem*! If you believe in your own abilities and have a favorable perception of yourself, you'll see positive results in your life. Self-esteem is a treasure that many people either lack completely or need to boost dramatically. If we could give all children just one gift — a gift they could keep with them to their final days — the best gift by far would be **self-esteem**, a strong belief in themselves. Self-esteem can do so much for the quality of your life. It's the springboard from which success is pursued and, eventually, reached. It's the starting point of your journey, the sustaining force that drives you, and the ultimate foundation for your achievements.

Parents play a vital role in developing and building their children's self-esteem. Children are impressionable creatures. Their primary role models (for better or worse) are their parents. I owe my own sense of self-worth to my mom and dad, who from day one have encouraged and supported me in every way. Since I can remember, they have believed in my God-given talents, abilities, and potential.

Two Life-Changing Gifts

But not everyone is blessed with an uplifting childhood and parents who whisper positive messages of reinforcement into their ears. Some people, unfortunately, suffer through years of insecurity and self-hatred before significant improvements take place.

A true example of triumph over such adversity is Dr. Leo Hennigan of Chevy Chase, Maryland. Dr. Leo, an 80-year-old retired psychiatrist and recovered alcoholic, was one of my students in a public speaking workshop. A member of Alcoholics Anonymous since 1963, he is also the author of a self-published book, *A Conspiracy of Silence: Alcoholism* (Gannel Publications, 1989), and a lecturer on the subject.

Dr. Leo spent more than half of his life carrying around a low self-image and a feeling of worthlessness. He never seemed to fit in socially as a child or as a young adult. His only means of escape (and temporary comfort) became drugs and alcohol. He gradually became more and more dependent on that extra drink to get him in a good mood. Over time, his dependency became an outright addiction.

As his condition worsened, his colleagues noticed his irrational and unpredictable behavior. But no one would confront him about his alcoholism — not even his doctor or his co-workers.

Dr. Leo explained to me that alcoholism was, and continues to be, a socially stigmatized disease. Many people sit back and watch as their family members and close friends sink into alcoholic dependency.

I asked Dr. Leo how he turned his life around, and what pivotal moments caused him to end his drug and alcohol addictions. He told me there were two moments that shaped his recovery and boosted his self-esteem. The first was when one of his closest friends and colleagues insinuated that if he didn't quit drinking he was going to lose his job. Dr. Leo had dedicated several years of his life to becoming a doctor. So he didn't want to sabotage his career through his self-destructive behavior. The other moment of hope was when one of Dr. Leo's close friends advised him that he should write a book about his experiences, and emphasized what a difference it could make in people's lives.

In the first case, someone had the courage to "tell it like it is" for Dr. Leo. In the second case, someone believed in him and helped him realize his own potential.

Dr. Leo has been sober for over 20 years. He is now spending his twilight years with his new wife, sharing his message with all who will listen that alcoholism is not a personal shortcoming or a flaw but, rather, a "disease of denial, apathy, and prejudice." Dr. Leo believes that the real breakthrough for alcoholics will come once we, as a society, eliminate the anonymity surrounding the disease.

Dr. Leo attributes his improvement in self-esteem to a woman who reached out to him and believed in him. When you face challenges that overwhelm you, reach out for help from those who care about you. Remember: Building your self-esteem can be a long process, but small, gradual improvements lead to bigger ones over time.

"You've gotta have a goal, a purpose."
– DR. LEO HENNIGAN

Four Ways to Boost Your Self-Image

Here are four ways to give your self-esteem a much-needed boost:

Surround yourself with positive, encouraging people. You may find that there are only two or three people close to you who fall under this category. That's OK! It's better to have just a few quality people in your life than to merely have superficial relationships with many people. You'll find comfort in knowing that you can turn to these people in your darkest hour, and that they'll listen to you without passing judgment.

When I was 11 years old and away at summer camp, I wrote a song about the importance of friendship and what it meant to me. The words stick with me to this day:

"Friends"

Friends are always there for you
And they will help you through and through

They never leave you helpless,
And they always care

They always show their kindness
Just by being there

Friends are special people
Who lend a helping hand

And the gift of love they give to you
Will help you understand

Sometimes you have to actively seek out positive, encouraging people, especially if you live and/or work in an unusually negative environment. It's hard to maintain a positive outlook on a regular basis when you receive constant negative feedback from the people around you.

One solution is to seek out a *mentor* — someone who is a bit older and wiser than you, and who can offer you time-tested advice and keep you on track with your personal and career objectives. (Kathleen Barton's recently published book — *Connecting with Success: How to Build a Mentoring Network to Fast-Forward Your Career* [Davies-Black Publishing, 2001] is an excellent guide on how you can find a mentor.) One of my greatest mentors is a man by the name of Larry Welch. Larry and I first met when I enrolled in one of his "Speechcraft" workshops, which are designed to help participants develop confidence in speaking before groups of people. From the first day we met, I marveled at Larry's ability to mobilize the efforts and spirits of others to get things done. He has given his time and expertise to support breast cancer survivors, aspiring public speakers, homeless people, prison inmates, underprivileged children, and others who are trying to make something of themselves.

One of Larry's most shining qualities is his ability to make other people feel good about themselves by teaching them to recognize their inner goodness and their potential for greatness. Larry has taught me to reach for high goals by the standards he has set for himself.

Sometimes your mentor will find you. In other cases, you and your mentor-to-be will stumble upon each other. Find as many mentors as you can to help you bring out your star-like qualities — the ones that will lead you to an abundant and fulfilling life.

Make daily affirmations. Each day, you should affirm and reaffirm to your subconscious mind that you are a worthwhile human being with gifts to offer the world; that you are unique; and that you can **do** or **become** anything you set your mind to, no matter what the obstacles.

Your subconscious mind will believe whatever you tell it if you do a good enough job of convincing it. The simplest way to do this is through **repetition** and **emphasis**. You also have to believe what you're saying — or at least act as though you believe it — and eventually you'll convince your subconscious mind that you can do whatever it is you're telling it you can do. Remember: When you make affirmations to yourself, speak with conviction.

Some examples of positive affirmations:

- "Everything I touch turns to gold."
- "I can do anything I put my mind to."
- "I am relentless! No one can stop me!"
- "I'm on my way to the top!"
- "Watch out world! Here I come!"
- "Good things are coming my way!"
- "I deserve the best, and I will get the best!"
- "I am me and I am okay. God don't make junk."

"Man lives by affirmation even more than he does by bread."
– VICTOR HUGO

When you make affirmations to yourself, you tap into an incredible personal power — the power of belief, the power of conviction, and the power of faith. I, for example, have said to myself many times (and believed): "I deserve the best, and I will get the best!" After allowing this belief to permeate my subconscious mind over time — through repetition and emphasis — a funny thing happened to me: I started attracting positive circumstances to my life. Just weeks after recovering from a failed romantic relationship, for example, I sat down and wrote some personal affirmations. I was determined to move forward and learn from my painful experience. Here's what I wrote:

- I resolve to live each day to the fullest.
- I resolve to listen to my inner voice for answers.
- I resolve to make the most of my talents.
- I resolve to learn from positive and negative experiences, and to move forward.

These simple affirmations of faith and hope helped me free myself of the pain of the past, and to open myself to new experiences of growth. Three weeks later, I met my future wife on a blind date. By affirming a new attitude about my future, I was able to improve my chances of meeting someone new instead of feeling sorry for myself.

So make your affirmations count: Let them express your deepest wishes and desires.

And don't be afraid to make affirmations to yourself on a daily basis. There's no such thing as a person who is too positive or who has too much motivation. Daily affirmations will keep you in an upbeat and resourceful state of mind, regardless of your circumstances. Self-motivation is powerful because you're able to give yourself inspiration and hope. You don't need to constantly rely on others to pronounce your greatness and potential. Instead, you can simply remind yourself of it regularly.

Think of some affirmations of your own and write them down below. Be sure to repeat them to yourself several times a day until their messages finally sink into your subconscious mind:

____

____

____

____

____

Focus on the "haves." Your attitude and self-image are strongly linked to what you focus on the most. If you dwell on what you're lacking in your life, or if you compare yourself to those who seem to have more or achieve more, your self-image will suffer.

To build a positive self-image, focus on the "haves" in your life: The friendships, partnerships, family bonds, talents, and unique gifts that bring joy to your life. In doing so, you'll pick yourself up when you're feeling down and become more compassionate toward people who are less fortunate than you.

Each night before I go to bed, I look up and thank the heavens above for what is **good** in my life. When I'm feeling overwhelmed, I say a prayer that Dr. Norman Vincent Peale wrote in his inspirational book, *The Power of Positive Thinking* (C.R. Gibson Company, 1970):

> "I believe this is going to be a wonderful day! I believe I can successfully handle all problems that will arise today! I feel good physically, mentally, and emotionally. It is wonderful to be alive! I am thankful for all that I have had, for all that I now have, and for all that I shall have. Things are not going to fall apart. God is here and He is with me and He will see me through. I thank God for every good thing."

Regardless of your religious beliefs — and even if you're not that religious or spiritual — reciting a prayer of thanks, with feeling and conviction, will improve your physical and emotional state almost immediately. No matter what's going on in your life, such a prayer helps to put things in perspective and restore your belief that everything **will** be OK.

Fall in love with yourself. You can't buy a positive self-image online. It isn't available at auction to the highest bidder. To develop a better relationship with yourself, you must learn to love who you are and appreciate your wonderful qualities!

Each day, think of one thing you like about yourself. For example, you might wake up, look in the mirror, and say: "I give 100 percent to my job. I always do my best!" Or you might be walking down the street when you realize that you have a knack for getting along with people — they like your sparkling personality! Or maybe you're a devoted parent and spouse, and your family looks up to you.

Recognizing your admirable attributes will enhance your personal and business relationships. People are naturally drawn to those who realize their own worth to their family, their organization, and/or their community. When you fall in love with yourself, other people will too. When you have a clear vision of your greatness, it becomes visible to everyone around you.

LIST SIX QUALITIES YOU LOVE ABOUT YOURSELF:

____

____

____

____

____

____

Integrity: Go for the "Gold"!

Educator Dale Carnegie, author of *How to Win Friends and Influence People* (Pocket Books, 1994), had a secret to a happy life — a secret that he said would put an end to at least half of your worries and create peace of mind:

> "I honestly believe that this is one of the greatest secrets to true peace of mind — a decent sense of values. And I believe we could annihilate fifty percent of all our worries at once if we would develop a sort of private gold standard — a gold standard of what things are worth to us in terms of our lives."

Carnegie's advice is simple yet powerful: Once we figure out "what things are worth to us in terms of our lives," we realize exactly how much value we place on the people around us as well as on our personal and career goals. In essence, we shape for ourselves a value system that serves as a guide for how to live our lives.

Four Practical Benefits of Living with Integrity

The best way to measure your success is by acknowledging who you touch and how you interact with others as you pursue your goals — in other words, your *integrity*. If you focus on positively affecting people's lives, you **will** make a difference.

Here are four ways that living with integrity will lead to true and lasting success:

You'll earn the trust and respect of others. We all know that trust and respect are valuable commodities that must be nurtured over a long period of time. When you treat others with respect and trust, you develop a reputation as a person of decency — and integrity. In turn, you gain the respect and trust of others, which will enrich your relationships with them. **Trust** and **respect** — two of my top five "relationship priorities" (see "Priorities — Know Your Bottom Line," below) — should be the cornerstones of any relationship, personal or professional. Can you imagine a business relationship in which each partner or company lacks respect for the other and fails to place its confidence in the other? That partnership would eventually dissolve into thin air!

You'll get what you give. I'm a firm believer in the "boomerang effect" — the idea that you reap what you sow in life. This concept dates back to biblical times. If you give 100 percent to everything you do — by valuing your relationships, honoring your commitments to others and to yourself, and holding yourself to the highest standards — good fortune will follow you throughout your life.

A shining example of this universal principle in action is Dottie Walters, founder and president of Walters International Speakers Bureau in Glendora, California, and publisher of *Sharing Ideas* magazine. Dottie's story of rising from poverty to international fame as a speaker/author is inspirational and heartwarming.

Dottie started out with no car, a rickety stroller for two babies, a borrowed typewriter and paper, and a high school education. She had served as features editor and ad manager of her high school newspaper, and she was determined that she and her high school sweetheart husband — who was back from the Second Marine Division after World War II — would not lose their small tract home.

There were few job opportunities in the recession that followed the war, so Dottie bought newspaper ad space on credit and created a "Shopper's Column" — all while she was building a second seat with bed pillows and clothesline rope on the back of her baby stroller and carrying extra cardboard in her purse to put in her worn-out shoes.

At the request of her advertisers, Dottie began building that advertising business into one of her own. Just one year later, she had 185 employees, four offices, and 4,000 annual contract advertisers. All this in a business typically dominated by men (especially at that time).

Since she was unable to find any books for women in sales at the library, she wrote one herself — *Never Underestimate the Selling Power of a*

Woman (Wilshire Book Company, 1986) — now a classic bestseller that was the first book of its kind. It's a guide that has inspired thousands of women around the world to follow Albert Einstein's advice: "Stop concentrating on problems. Focus on solutions!"

Throughout Dottie's 30 years in business, she has shared her expertise via speaking around the world and writing books and articles to inspire others to pursue their dreams. She often quotes, and hears the voices of, her "friends of the mind" — historical figures like Benjamin Franklin, Amelia Earhart, and George Washington Carver, all of whom have "spoken" to her through biographies and other literature.

Today, Dottie receives thousands of letters of love and praise from adoring and appreciative businesspeople, authors, and clients around the world who have benefited from her seminars, keynotes, books and tapes, and media interviews. Her wisdom, experience, and eagerness to help others grow their own businesses are known around the globe. She turns on the lights of the mind for thousands of aspiring speakers, entrepreneurs, and writers, and she's achieved financial and professional success for herself and her family as a result.

Dottie is famous for quoting her poor, immigrant Scottish grandfather, who told her when she was a small child:

> "If you are hurt, you may have to lie down and bleed a wee bit, lassie. But you will **get up again**!"

She puts her fingertips on her wrist, as her grandfather taught her, to feel the Scottish "drums" drumming, and she hears in her heart the skirl of the "bagpipes" calling, "Get up!"

You'll be able to live with yourself. Essential to personal growth and fulfillment is a clear, honest assessment of yourself. It takes courage to look yourself square in the eyes and acknowledge your true feelings and motives. Only when we're honest with ourselves can we have true peace of mind. As my mom always says to me, borrowing Shakespeare's golden words: "To thine own self be true."

So ask yourself why you've chosen a particular career path or why you're thinking about heading in a certain direction. Make sure the reasons for your actions are ones you can live with. For instance, are you taking a job at the local auto shop because your friend expects you to? Or are you going to law school because you're next "in line" in a family of lawyers?

A moment of truth came for me one week before I was scheduled to take the entrance examination for law school. I met with a career counselor who asked me, simply, "Why do you want to go to law school?" A simple enough question, right? Well, I was dumbfounded by the fact that I couldn't give a decent response. I then realized that I'd been going through the motions and following the "crowd mentality," since many of my friends had been planning to go to law school.

During our session, the counselor advised me **not** to take the entrance exam unless I was 100 percent sure I wanted to go to law school. After our conversation, I realized — with relief — that a career in law was not the path for me.

By being truly honest about my feelings, I was able to admit that I wasn't sure what the future would hold for me — but that I **had** ruled out a career as a lawyer. Narrowing your options by asking tough questions of yourself will help you move closer to finding your true calling in life.

You'll be more likely to follow your own path. Have you ever had the experience of other people telling you what you **can** and **can't** do in life? what you **should** or **shouldn't** do? what your limitations are? Perhaps you've been trying to live your father's dream of becoming a doctor, even though you have minimal interest in medicine. Or maybe your family has come to expect that you will follow a certain path they've carved out for you — go to college, get your degree, find a well-paying job, and settle down and get married in a nice house right down the street.

You may find yourself living according to other people's expectations for your life. My advice is simple: **Don't do it**! Be a trailblazer. Find and follow your own path. It takes courage to go against the grain of what people expect of you, but you can do it! Parents in some cultures, for example, **expect** their children to adhere to a certain way of life and to "inherit" the family business or to follow in the footsteps of previous generations of family members. Arranged marriages and pre-determined careers can put you into a bind that is difficult to escape. But you owe it to yourself to do what makes **you** happy. After all, you're the one expending the effort. It's your life, to live the way **you** choose.

When I graduated from college, some people close to me figured I would pursue a high-paying job (or at least a paying job!). But, recognizing a great opportunity when I see one, I decided — against popular opinion — to take an unpaid internship at the U.S. Department of Justice in the Office of International Affairs. I worked 40 hours a week for no pay.

My inner voice had been telling me to take the opportunity, regardless of the naysayers. But I was also determined to live on my own, be independent, and support myself financially. So I found a job as a bellman at a local hotel. I put in 65-hour work weeks, getting paid for just 25 of those hours.

Intern by day, bellman by night — I was determined to do whatever it took to gain valuable internship experience while still making enough money to support myself. I refused to live the life others wanted for me. I wanted to find and follow my own path. You should too! When you follow your own path, you'll experience the joy of making your own mistakes, learning your own lessons, and achieving your own successes.

Priorities: Know Your Bottom Line

You must decide what you **do** and **do not** want out of life! Take control of a relationship, for example, by deciding what you want out of it. What qualities are most important to you in another person? Exactly what will you tolerate from or in someone else? How much of yourself are you willing to invest in a relationship?

Or look at your career: What type of work do you want to do? What kind of organization can you see yourself working for? Maybe you want to work for yourself instead. Home-based, one-person businesses are a fast-growing trend in America. Determine exactly how much money you want to earn each year, how many hours per week you want to work, and what kind of people you want to work with and for.

Make a list of what you do and do not want in your life. It's an exercise that will force you to take a profound look at your wants and needs. When asked what they're looking for in a relationship or a job, many people reply, "I don't know what I want." Don't be among the "priority-challenged." Take inventory of yourself!

Relationships

Here are five of my relationship-related **do wants** and **don't wants**:

WHAT I DO WANT	*WHAT I DON'T WANT*
1) Communication	1) Dishonesty
2) Appreciation	2) Jealousy
3) Respect	3) Negativity
4) Trust	4) Mistrust
5) Relationship is No. 1 priority	5) Disloyalty

What are your relationship-related **do wants** and **don't wants**?

WHAT I DO WANT	*WHAT I DON'T WANT*
1. ______	1. ______
2. ______	2. ______
3. ______	3. ______
4. ______	4. ______
5. ______	5. ______

Now that you have a clear idea of what you **do** and **do not** want in a relationship, you've taken an important first step toward improved self-awareness, and you'll be able to identify someone with most (if not all) of the qualities you seek. Let this information be your personal "measuring bar" in your relationships.

Career

Here are five of my career-related **do wants** and **don't wants**:

WHAT I DO WANT	*WHAT I DON'T WANT*
1) Involves various people	1) Isolation from others
2) To use my "gift of gab"	2) To be money-driven
3) A service-oriented job	3) The same routine
4) Challenge and excitement	4) Someone else's path
5) To inspire and educate	5) To take the easy way

What are your career-related **do wants** and **don't wants**?

WHAT I DO WANT	*WHAT I DON'T WANT*
1. ______	1. ______
2. ______	2. ______
3. ______	3. ______

4. ______________________	4. ______________________
5. ______________________	5. ______________________

Figure out precisely what you're looking for and what you want to avoid in your career. How else will you land the job of your dreams? How else will you find work that fulfills you and brings you joy and satisfaction?

One of the finest reference guides available on the subject of career choices is *What Color Is Your Parachute?* (Ten Speed Press, 2002), by Richard Nelson Bolles, a book that is quite unique in that it is updated and revised each year. Bolles's book is an excellent resource for people who are seeking to change careers; identify their job-related skills, interests, and values; and determine their optimal career path. In *Parachute*, Bolles points out the following troubling statistic:

> Surveys of worker dissatisfaction find that up to 80%, or four out of every five, workers are dissatisfied with some important aspect of their jobs or careers.

Perhaps a major reason for this rampant frustration in the workplace is that people avoid taking the time to determine what they **really** want out of life — what **really** fires them up. But **you** don't have to settle for whatever situation you may be stuck in now. No matter how bleak your circumstances may appear, there is always a way out! To find it, however, you need to look inside yourself. So make a "wish list" for your ideal job. Then go out and find — or create — the job that meets your wish list's requirements. Don't stop until you're completely content with what you're doing.

My sister Susan has had lots of experience in the hospitality industry. It has always seemed to be her cup of tea. Her animated personality and her ability to get along with other people have consistently served her well. But a while back, she started to feel that something was noticeably missing in her life. She had a continuing sense that she wasn't achieving her full potential — that there was so much more she could be doing with her life.

Susan's first priority was to change her lifestyle. "I'm tired of working nights and weekends, having no social life and no time to do anything for myself," she said. "Baby, it's time for days!" So she found a new job as a manager, through which she could challenge herself and meet new people. In the process, she freed up her nights and weekends so that she could have a life outside of work. By taking a careful, detailed inventory of her needs and wants (and her don't needs and don't wants!), she was able to make a satisfying transition.

Our careers and relationships directly determine the quality of our lives. What we do all day long and who we interact with are personal choices. Choose carefully and you will find great joy in your life.

"Whatever you can do,
or dream you can, begin it.
Boldness has genius, power,
and magic in it. Begin it now!"
— JOHANN WOLFGANG VON GOETHE

GIVE YOURSELF A GREAT REPUTATION TO LIVE UP TO

Once you've set some exciting and challenging goals, you need to start telling people about them. Why? Because when you "publicize" your goals, you force yourself to set your ideas into motion. Telling someone else about your goals transforms your mind from a state of inertia to a state of action. Suddenly your goals, which were once just ideas, begin to take shape and develop a life of their own — because now you've given yourself a great reputation to live up to! And as your goals become more specific, you're better able to form a concrete plan to achieve them — and then turn that plan into reality:

IDEA → GOAL → PLAN → REALITY

One magical and powerful idea can transform itself into reality through the dynamic process of goal setting and detailed planning. Take, for example, this book. The idea for the book came to me in the middle of the night a full three years before its publication. Fortunately I had the good sense to write my brainstorm down on an index card. I scribbled the word "success" and then turned it into an acronym, with each letter representing its own word. Together the words spelled out a process for becoming successful over and over again in your life — and they thus became the foundation for the chapters in this book.

Several months later, I set a goal to write the book I had in mind — one that would focus on the process I had outlined and the principles involved in successful living. I announced my goal in front of a large group of friends one evening to "make it official." And less than a week later I began writing down my ideas and doing the research that led to the creation of the book you now hold in your hands.

When you formally declare your goals to the people around you, and commit yourself to achieving them, conditions and circumstances will begin to work in your favor.

POINTS TO REMEMBER

- Choose the right goals — ones that match **your** values.
- Find a healthy balance among your goals.
- Be accountable for your actions and attitudes.
- Develop (or refine) a personal mission statement.
- Take a "SIP" of success — ***Self-esteem***, ***Integrity***, and ***Priorities***

TWO

UNDERSTAND

Conquer Emotional Clutter

"Of all knowledge, the wise and good seek most to know themselves."

— WILLIAM SHAKESPEARE

Before we can begin the process of pursuing our goals and aspirations, we need to recognize and eliminate emotional barriers that stand in our way and prevent us from making progress. What will it take to get **you** moving in the direction of your dreams? What will you have to do to get from where you are (the status quo) to where you want to be? And what are you willing to sacrifice in order to make it all happen?

Success is rarely an overnight phenomenon. Instead, "sudden fame and fortune" is usually the result of months or even years of dedication and persistence. I've found *persistence* to be the most important element of a successful life. Intelligence, wealth, and talent are helpful; but what matters more in the long run is a burning desire for continuous self-improvement. Virgil said that "fortune favors the bold." But fortune also has a keen eye for people who are dedicated to and passionate about their unique purpose in life.

DISCOVER THE SOURCE OF YOUR GREATNESS

There is one source of power, knowledge, and strength that is **universal**. What is this source? Is it some wise, old guru meditating on a remote mountaintop? Is it a special lamp housing a genie who makes your every wish come true? Is it some mysterious, prehistoric charm that, when touched, radiates enormous power and energy?

No! The universal source of power lies largely untapped in the human spirit, deep inside each and every one of us! Often, this power lies dormant and remains hidden to us. But if you're willing to learn more about yourself — to **Understand** yourself better — you can discover how to tap into your spirit and identify talents, abilities, and potential you never knew you had. Inside you, and everyone, lie the seeds of **greatness** and **superstardom**.

What makes people like Benjamin Franklin, Rev. Dr. Martin Luther King, Jr., Susan B. Anthony, or Mother Teresa different from us? Not much! "Ordinary" people can and do become **extraordinary** people! These particular people recognized the power that originated within them. Their awareness of their true selves and their real purposes allowed them to make extraordinary contributions to society.

Imagine an Extraordinary Life

A real-life example of someone who turned ordinary skills into extraordinary success is Derek Jeter, shortstop for the New York Yankees. In his book *The Life You Imagine: Life Lessons for Achieving Your Dreams* (Crown Publishers, 2001), Jeter shares the inspiring story of his humble upbringing in Kalamazoo, Michigan, and his gradual transformation from a skinny kid with a big dream to an All-Star player for a World Series-winning baseball dynasty.

From his earliest memories as a child, Jeter always envisioned himself as a professional baseball player for the New York Yankees. His goal was definite. His dream was etched in his subconscious mind. Every day, he did something to take him one small step closer to his vision of greatness. He knew from the very beginning that he had within himself the power to make his dream come true.

According to Jeter — whose "office" is Yankee Stadium and whose paycheck is over $10 million a year — to achieve your vision, you must be 100 percent dedicated to your dream. You have to believe in yourself even when no one else does — even when you begin to doubt yourself. Jeter knows of what he speaks. As an 18-year-old minor league draftee of the New York Yankees, he initially felt like an outsider on a team of seasoned pros, and he sometimes wondered if he really had what it takes to become a professional ballplayer. Some nights, after a particularly poor performance, he'd go back to his room and cry himself to sleep. But after each setback, whether it be a hitless doubleheader or an error-laden afternoon, he would focus on the one or two things he'd done right — and then work on becoming even better at them.

Jeter says he would never have achieved his dream without his mom and dad, sister, and close friends and mentors, who all challenged him to be his best and believed in his vision of future greatness.

You, too, can live the life you imagine — if you're willing to improve on your weaknesses and build on your strengths, and if you're willing to change and grow as your dream gets closer to fruition.

Learn Continuously

Life is one giant class, beginning at birth and lasting anywhere from a few minutes to several decades. None of us knows how long our own class will last. So we must each resolve to learn as much as we can before the final bell rings.

You will have many instructors during your classroom instruction. Some will be parents, schoolteachers, older siblings, law enforcement officers, scoutmasters, politicians, or clergy. Other instructors will take the form of romantic and business relationships, the death of a loved one, separation or loss of a relationship, competition with others and yourself, rejection, the pursuit of a dream, or conversations with older folks who have already learned many of life's lessons.

You'll also take many field trips throughout your class session. You may visit a foreign land, learn a new language and discover a new culture. You might spend some time on a college campus with others your age, working to form lasting friendships and to pursue new knowledge and ideas. Perhaps you'll even walk down an aisle and devote yourself to another person, committing yourself to enriching his or her life and enhancing his or her personal growth.

But you might also find yourself at the bedside of a loved one who is stricken with a terminal illness. Or maybe you'll be entrenched on a battlefield, fighting to protect your country as well as yourself and your comrades. Or perhaps you'll be locked in a courtroom battle with your ex-, arguing over custody rights where your children are concerned.

Ultimately, no matter what circumstances we find ourselves in, we learn valuable lessons through our experiences (good and bad). All of our experiences teach us something about ourselves. And when we learn more about ourselves, our lives become richer and more meaningful. We're better equipped for the rest of our journey. As one of my favorite sayings puts it: "If you are not learning, you are not living!"

"The unexamined life is not worth living."
— SOCRATES

SELF-EXAMINATION

A clear, honest assessment of yourself is critical to your long-term success. Acknowledging your strengths helps you build confidence in yourself and produce the results you want in life. At the same time, recognizing your weak points allows you to work on areas of your personality or behavior that prevent you from making necessary changes in your life — areas you would have otherwise ignored had you not focused on improving them.

So identify your strengths and weaknesses. What are your sparkling attributes? What qualities do you possess that you would seek in others? Which of your characteristics shine brightly and make the world a better place? Conversely, what areas of your life need a touch-up? How can you be more effective and productive?

I'll go first! Let's see …

STRENGTHS	*AREAS TO IMPROVE*
people-oriented	become a better listener
self-confident	become more organized
trustworthy	become more punctual
independent spirit	become more accountable for my actions
compassionate	control my emotions better

What does **your** balance sheet look like?

STRENGTHS	*AREAS TO IMPROVE*
________________	________________
________________	________________
________________	________________
________________	________________
________________	________________

Sometimes we are too close to our own behavior to recognize what we're doing right and where we're going astray. So in addition to examining yourself and your own actions, you should also seek out an objective viewpoint from someone whose opinion you value.

For example, while I consider myself to be a very good husband — faithful, kind, and thoughtful — I'm certainly not perfect. I recently asked my wife to tell me one of my greatest strengths as a spouse and one of my greatest weaknesses as well. Starting with the good news, she told me I never let a day go by without telling her at least a dozen times that I love her. On the flip side, she gently pointed out that I have a tendency to leave my clothes on the floor when I'm really tired instead of putting them in the hamper. This had become a weakness for me — not disciplining myself to toss the clothes into the hamper.

Having someone else point out your strengths **and** your weaknesses may be uncomfortable at first. But it will give you the opportunity to "make good" on your bad habits or errant behaviors and resolve your problems. And it just might help you pinpoint strengths you never knew you had!

In his bestselling book *Don't Sweat the Small Stuff … and It's All Small Stuff* (Hyperion, 1997), author Richard Carlson offers several tips on how to live a more peaceful, relaxed life. One of his suggestions is to "acknowledge the totality of your being." We should accept ourselves as we are, flaws and all, Carlson asserts. When we become aware of our faults and imperfections, he notes, we also become aware of our strong points and qualities, creating a complete picture of who we are.

When we develop a heightened level of self-awareness, we awaken ourselves to our **true** selves — to the essence of who we really are! This is the heart of self-esteem: Accepting ourselves exactly as we are.

Emotional Check-up

Our emotions play a huge role in promoting or hindering our success. Many times they impede us instead of helping us reach our goals. Whenever we suppress our feelings — or dwell on them for too long — we allow ourselves to collect emotional "debris," which then gets in the way of our personal growth.

How can you clear the emotional debris from your life? Here are five strategies you can use:

Release the "Demons"

You may have "demons" welling up inside you right now! They can go by various names, like "guilt," "anger," "fear," "frustration," and "anxiety." If unchecked, these demons can pull you down, hold you back, eat you alive, or even kill you!

There's **good** news, however: You can vanquish these demons! Doing so requires both courage and the willingness to face your problems head on. Once you realize how these demons are adversely affecting your life, you'll see how much better your life will be without them.

Here are the five demons that are most likely to do you in, emotionally speaking:

Demon 1: Guilt. Guilt can plague your soul like nothing else can! It causes you to behave out of a false sense of obligation. It's your conscience telling you you've been "bad," and that, therefore, you deserve punishment of some kind. Guilt destroys your self-esteem! It demoralizes you and crushes your spirit!

Bulimics — people who "binge" on large amounts of food and then make themselves throw it all up immediately afterward — often suffer from guilt. They feel bad about themselves and the way they look, so they eat. Then they feel guilty about what they've done, so they purge what they've eaten. This vicious cycle continues in a downward spiral until the person's physical and emotional health are both in jeopardy.

Guilt is most often a self-imposed demon. Others might not blame you or look down upon you, but you carry around enough self-blame for an army! I, for example, can clearly recall one time from my youth when I carried around a tremendous amount of guilt. I was away on a winter camping trip with the Boy Scouts. We stayed in a big log cabin and played a lot of outdoor sports like touch football, capture the flag, and freeze tag. At one point, some of us started a game to see who had the best arm for throwing stones up in the trees.

Being of a competitive nature, I threw my share of rocks up in those trees! The problem was that it was difficult to see the rocks coming back down. Not long after we started the game, I reached back, flung a stone sky high, and then watched it land right on the head of one of the other Scouts. His head started bleeding profusely. I was petrified! What if I had killed him?! Oh no! Why had I thrown those rocks anyway?! I felt absolutely queasy all afternoon.

The boy ended up being just fine — but that didn't stop me from feeling terrible about the incident. I apologized to the boy and to my leaders for doing something I shouldn't have been doing in the first place. Although the boy and the leaders forgave me, I had trouble forgiving myself. Guilty feelings lingered for a few weeks before I was finally able to mentally put that near-tragedy to rest. The hardest part of the "guilt process" is not always receiving forgiveness from others, but learning to stop blaming **yourself**.

Strategies for Overcoming Guilt

- Acknowledge your guilty feelings and determine their original causes.
- Realize how the guilt is decreasing the quality of your life and overtaking you.
- Consider how much better your life would be if the burden of guilt were lifted.
- Resolve to learn from your mistake(s) and become a better person.

Demon 2: Anger. Anger is incredibly destructive. It can destroy friendships, it can destroy family ties, and it can destroy **you**! It can lead you to say or do things you'll probably regret right after saying or doing them. Let's face it: Anger does serious harm to everyone involved. The person who lashes out often ends up feeling ashamed and embarrassed, while the victim of the anger is left with open wounds in the form of hurt feelings and a damaged ego.

"God don't make junk." I have a friend I'll call "Alice." Alice was physically and emotionally abused as a child. Her biological father repeatedly told her that she was worthless and would never amount to much in life.

To avoid confrontation with her father, Alice would hide herself in a closet. She needed an escape, a safe harbor from the chaos of her family life — a life that consisted of name-calling, threats, and endless emotional upheaval.

Growing up, Alice was told by teachers and guidance counselors that she would never go to college. Her schoolmates used to tease her because of her unusual accent. For a brief period, her family was homeless and was forced to live in a campground.

Alice has overcome many obstacles, however, despite the rough conditions of her childhood. Fortunately she had a loving mother by her side, who told her, "God don't make junk, and you're not junk!" As hard as it was for Alice to believe those words, her mom repeatedly told her she was a worthwhile human being who had a lot to offer to the world.

Alice eventually went on to college to continue her studies. She ignored the people who had said she couldn't do it.

Just three days before her scheduled graduation, she was told she couldn't walk across the stage with her classmates and receive her degree because her grades weren't good enough. But instead of getting angry and wallowing in despair, Alice accepted the disappointment and took two classes over the summer to boost her grades.

Alice didn't receive her diploma with all of her classmates, surrounded by pomp and circumstance. Then again, she did have her **own** pomp and circumstance: She was surrounded by family members and neighbors as the postman delivered her diploma to her front door. She graciously accepted it and gave the postman a big hug. Soon after, she went on to teach special education at a prestigious private school, where she continues to enrich the lives of young children with special needs to this day.

Alice had as much reason to feel angry as anyone, and for a while she **was** angry. Over time, though, she learned to deal with her anger by acknowledging her feelings and tracing them back to her physical and emotional abuse as a child. By taking this courageous first step, Alice put herself on the road to releasing this demon from her life — after having harbored rage and frustration for so many years.

"The Raging Storm"

The storms rage inside of me.

The anger takes over,
and I don't know what to do.
I feel as if I don't know where else to turn.

The lightning flashes before my eyes.

I am blinded by the light that flashes,
frightening flashes of hurt and anger.

Why do I hurt? Why am I so angry?

I feel so alone when I am hurt and angry.

I hurt others when I am hurt and angry.

I don't want this anymore.

I don't want the storms anymore.
I want sunshine.
I will control my anger so I see rainbows.
– Anonymous

Eventually, Alice came to realize the destructive toll anger was taking on her life. Her intimate relationships and friendships had all suffered because of her built-up hostility. But though she understood how much better off she'd be without the anger, she didn't know how to get rid of it. Even several years of counseling didn't seem to help.

One day, I sat down with Alice, looked her squarely in the eyes, and asked her to forgive her father for what he had done, and to forgive all those who had torn down her self-esteem, directly or indirectly, over the years. She burst into tears. In all her years of counseling, no one had ever suggested forgiveness as a possible solution. Everyone had been quick to blame people or circumstances.

After some time, Alice took a brave step forward and decided to forgive her father and all those who had emotionally harmed her throughout her life. Suddenly, an incredible burden was lifted off her shoulders. She had ridden herself of the anger by developing the courage to forgive. It wasn't easy for her to do, mind you. But once she saw how much she'd benefit from such an act, she was eager to see it through.

Alice is now able to truly pursue her dreams, boldly and passionately! By conquering the powerful demon of **anger**, she has literally transformed her life. Getting rid of all the anger and resentment has bolstered her self-confidence, opened her up to love and happiness, and given her true and lasting peace of mind.

If you allow anger to fester inside you, its path of destruction may include:

- destroyed relationships,
- any number of health problems,
- added and undue tension and anxiety,
- regretful words that can't be taken back,
- physically or emotionally harmful behavior,
- coldness and indifference, and/or
- an early grave.

Strategies for Overcoming Anger

- Acknowledge your feelings of anger, resentment, and hostility and get to the root of those feelings.
- Identify the adverse effects anger is having on your life — e.g., poor health, insomnia, isolation, severed relationships.
- Consider the benefits of living without anger. Among them: Improved health, better relationships, more peace of mind.
- Make an effort to forgive regardless of whether the other person takes responsibility for his or her actions. Remember: You're only responsible for **your** attitude.

Demon 3: Fear. Fear, at its worst, can paralyze you and prevent you from leading a normal life. Fear destabilizes and immobilizes you! Its grip can be relentless — and its outcome fatal.

Entire nations have been immobilized by fear: Fear of death, fear to speak out and voice opinions, fear to be oneself, fear to lead a normal life. The real crippling effect of fear is that it prevents you from moving forward and taking action to achieve your true potential. Perhaps that's why Eleanor Roosevelt once said, "Fear is the most devastating emotion on earth." Mrs. Roosevelt learned to conquer her fears by helping others. This strategy proved to be tremendously therapeutic for her because it took her mind off her own problems and worries. She soon forgot about her own concerns and lost the self-consciousness she'd fought for years.

Various surveys have shown that fear of public speaking is one of the most common fears Americans have. Yet public speaking is one of the most important skills one can possibly acquire. Most people will be required to speak before an audience, great or small, at some point in their lives. Perhaps you, for example, will be asked to give a toast at a banquet or celebration. Or maybe you'll have to give a speech or formal presentation to a class. Or maybe you'll be asked to facilitate a business meeting. Or perhaps you might be chosen to give a eulogy for a friend or family member. There are innumerable opportunities to speak before others, and your time will eventually come.

Does that scare you? Well, you're not alone. I've found that the best and most effective way to overcome this fear is to practice speaking in a nonthreatening, supportive environment, such as Toastmasters International or a Speaking Circles group. The key to alleviating your public speaking jitters is to focus on your message and the occasion instead of your performance. Ask for feedback from your "circle of support" and continue speaking at every opportunity. Consistent practice in a nurturing environment will rapidly improve your speaking skills and diminish your fear.

Outlive your fears. A true example of triumph over the fear of public speaking is Linda Schultz, a civilian employee of the Department of the Navy in Washington, D.C. Linda suffered for most of her adult life from a crippling fear of speaking in front of an audience. The mere thought of addressing a group of people on any subject — formal or intimate — absolutely petrified her. She understood, though, that if she continued to live in fear of speaking, she'd miss out on important opportunities in her personal life and in her career.

Determined to conquer her fear, Linda joined Toastmasters International, a worldwide organization whose mission is to help people become better listeners, speakers, and leaders. As she was about to make her "ice breaker" speech, which she had already postponed a half-dozen times, Linda approached the lectern with cue cards in hand and delivered her entire five-minute speech with her white-knuckled hands firmly gripping the edges of the lectern. Linda doesn't recall a word she said during her "inaugural" speech, but she does remember the relief she felt once it was all over.

Linda received encouraging feedback from her peers, and she continued giving prepared presentations, each time with less fear and more eagerness. In the past four years, Linda has delivered several dozen presentations, coached and trained aspiring public speakers, and learned to feel relaxed and comfortable addressing an audience of any size. Linda was able to "outlive" her fear of public speaking by realizing she needed to make a change — and by acknowledging that the only way she could enjoy more opportunities for success was to approach her fear and conquer it.

We all have fears and worries that prevent us from taking the steps required to live the life we desire. Consistent action toward your goals, however — often one "baby step" at a time — will help you reduce the paralyzing effects of fear, and maybe even "outlive" them.

Strategies for Conquering Excessive Fear

- Acknowledge your fears and try to pinpoint their causes.
- Think about the destructive toll these fears are taking on your life.
- Consider the benefits of living without the fears or, even better, using the fears to your advantage.
- Prepare for the worst-case scenario, then approach your fear with confidence, knowing it can't get any worse.

"If you persuade yourself that you can do a certain thing, provided this thing be possible, you will do it, however difficult it may be. If, on the contrary, you imagine you cannot do the simplest thing in the world, it is impossible for you to do it, and molehills become for you unscalable mountains."
– ÉMILE COUÉ

Demon 4: Frustration. It's very easy to get frustrated in life. Things don't go exactly as planned. You're in a rut. Or you're in a dead-end job with no chance for advancement. Or you're stuck in an unfulfilling relationship with the "person of your nightmares" instead of the "person of your dreams."

Maybe you're among the many people in this world who feel miserable because their lives lack fulfillment and excitement. Perhaps you feel like you're drifting aimlessly through life, allowing your dreams to fade away and eventually disappear. If so, you're bound to be frustrated — because you realize that you're not pursuing your dreams and living up to your fullest potential.

Anytime you decide to stretch yourself and make drastic changes in your life, you will inevitably encounter obstacles — and get frustrated — along the way. The key to dealing with your frustration is to learn how to handle the setbacks you experience and prevent them from throwing you off course. You can do this by viewing your setbacks as challenges — as opportunities to use the creative power of your imagination.

Mark Fisher, author of *The Millionaire's Secrets* (Fireside, 1997), advises us to regard each day as a new life that is full of hope and new opportunities:

> "Cultivate in yourself the ability to forget your past frustrations. Clean the slate. Your life begins anew each day. Your determination grows stronger each day, and you approach a success you never dreamed possible. Just persevere."

This philosophy captures an extraordinary way to remove needless frustration and anxiety from your life. Simply regard each day as a fresh start

— as a chance to redeem yourself and start anew. Learn from your past mistakes, of course, but retain only the **lessons**, not the **frustrations**.

Former U.S. President Harry S Truman found this type of strategy to be an effective tool for dealing with election frustration. On the eve of Election Day in 1948, while the whole country — including his own wife — was anticipating his loss, Truman decided to put an end to the day and go to bed. Tomorrow, he thought to himself, he would wake up and start a new day. The sun would rise and so would hope and victory. The next day the newspapers read: "Dewey Defeats Truman!" But in actuality, the opposite was true: Truman had rallied from behind (thanks to last-minute support from voters) and won the election, surprising himself, his colleagues, Dewey, and the nation!

You won't always have the same fortune Truman had, of course. But you will find that, by taking life one chunk at a time instead of biting off more than you can chew, you'll be in a better frame of mind to cope with the inevitable challenges and hurdles you'll face — and the frustrations they'll occasionally cause.

A stranger to the word "failure." A former colleague of mine, Michael, knows the crippling effects of excessive frustration. Michael was born with a learning disability and several other psychological difficulties. He was also the victim of sexual and emotional abuse throughout his childhood. Educational achievement just didn't seem to be in the stars for him. Friends, counselors, and teachers told Michael that he didn't have the mental capacity to graduate from high school, and that he'd never have the luxury of being employed in the "real world."

Fortunately, Michael didn't leave his future in the hands of other people's opinions. He struggled to deal with a stuttering problem and the distractions of his family life. Four times he failed the test that would qualify him to graduate from high school, but he hung in there and gave it one more try. On his fifth attempt, with the help of an encouraging teacher who believed in him and his potential for a productive life, Michael passed the exam and was able to call himself a high school graduate. He had achieved a dream that many people take for granted. Other people had told him he couldn't do it — but he did it anyway!

Soon after graduation, Michael landed a job at a reputable law firm. He is now surpassing many people's expectations — including his own in some cases. Michael has refused to let frustration keep him down, and he attributes his success to his refusal to believe in failure or defeat.

An angel confronts her demons. Your emotional life can take a turn for the worst when you allow frustrations to build up inside of you. Most of our problems are temporary and reversible. With time, persistence, and the support of others, our situations will usually improve. But frustration has a way of compounding itself and, if unchecked, it can ruin your life — and perhaps even end it.

My sister-in-law, Christian Victoria "Chrissie" Carrigan, who became "my little sis," endured various degrees of frustration during her relatively short time on earth. Born three months premature and weighing just 2 pounds, 5 1/2 ounces, Chrissie was hospitalized and in an incubator for the first three months of her life.

Chrissie spent the first few months out of the hospital in critical condition. She made frequent trips back to the hospital and was connected to an apnea monitor and an oxygen tank for the first year and a half of her life. Chrissie's parents enrolled her in the Infants in Transition program at the Ivymount School in Rockville, Maryland, where she received physical and occupational therapy. Since she was unable to speak for the first two and a half years of her life, Chrissie's primary means of human interaction was sign language. Her preschool teachers used "total communication" techniques, combining pictures, vocal and sign language to educate her.

During her toddler years, Chrissie developed acute asthma, along with severe allergies resulting from her premature birth. In the second grade, she suffered from auditory processing dysfunction. By the fifth grade, her peripheral vision and short-term memory had begun to diminish. Due to her many physical challenges, she missed an entire year of school, receiving specialized instruction at home.

Life was a constant physical struggle for Chrissie. Yet, somehow, she managed to thrive in her studies, despite the many physical and mental challenges she faced. Chrissie faced her greatest challenges in her freshman and sophomore years of high school, when she became severely depressed and developed anorexia nervosa — a life-threatening eating disorder. Her depression and anorexia triggered Multiple Personality Disorder, a condition in which five very strong, conflicting personalities battled one another for control of Chrissie.

One evening, after months of self-defeating thoughts and private journal entries in which she contemplated suicide, one of Chrissie's personalities took over and caused her to take her own life. She had just turned 15 a few weeks earlier. The pain from her personal battles was just too much for her to bear. She felt there was no way out.

I and the rest of our family are now left wondering, "Why did this have to happen?" "Why Chrissie? Why now? Why ever? Why did she feel there was no way out? Why couldn't we do anything to prevent it?" After reading three years' worth of Chrissie's journal entries, we now truly understand the nature of the daily battles that waged within her. Shortly after her death, Chrissie's mom described her in her final days as "an old soul in a young girl's body."

According to the American Foundation of Suicide Prevention (AFSP), suicide is the eighth-leading cause of death in America today, and the third-leading cause of death in young adults between the ages of 15 and 24. The AFSP also notes that there are approximately 764,000 suicide attempts in America each year. Over 5 million living Americans have tried to take their own life at some point. The AFSP reminds family members and friends who are left behind that "suicide is caused by illness. It is not a character flaw or a sign of weakness."

If you know someone who has committed suicide, an excellent resource and coping manual is *After Suicide*, by John H. Hewett (The Westminster Press, 1980). This book provides answers to grief-stricken survivors on how to cope with life after the loss of a loved one through suicide — how to sift through the various emotions, such as guilt, anger, and shock, all emotions that naturally follow such a life-changing event.

In Chrissie's own way, she became an angel of inspiration. Just six days after her death, Douglas Duncan — the county executive for Montgomery County, Maryland — declared December 12, 2001, "Chrissie Carrigan Day." The proclamation celebrated Chrissie's miraculous life and her special gifts, which included poetic and artistic ability; her academic achievement as an Honor Roll student; and her compassion for wildlife, nature, and endangered species. Chrissie had aspired to one day become a child psychologist, in the hopes of helping teenagers cope with the very same eating disorders she was trying to overcome.

Chrissie touched the lives of many, but none more than her older sister — my wife, Trevia — who changed career paths (from veterinary science to early childhood special education) as a result of watching Chrissie's early struggles with special needs. Because of Chrissie's difficulties, Trevia realized that her "calling" was to make a difference in the lives of young children with special needs.

Chrissie's brain has been donated to the University of Maryland for research on the causes and effects of depression — and its relationship with suicide. An annual memorial scholarship has been started in her name to assist graduating seniors of Northwest High School in Germantown, Maryland. An annual "Chrissie's Angel Fun Run" is being planned to help support her scholarship fund.

Chrissie's frustrations ended her life, but her untimely death has taught many people the importance of reaching out for help before it's too late. The loss of Chrissie has left a gap in the hearts of our family. But we believe that, in time, that "gap" will once again be filled by Chrissie's spirit, which is already manifesting itself in the positive actions of others who have been affected by her death.

"Every adversity, every failure,
and every heartache carries with it
the Seed of an equivalent
or greater Benefit."
— NAPOLEON HILL

Strategies for Overcoming Frustration

- Acknowledge your feelings of frustration and examine their causes.
- Realize how frustration is holding you back from fulfilling your dreams.
- Consider how much better your life would be without unnecessary frustrations.
- Reach out and ask for guidance from someone who is both **willing** and **able** to help you.

Demon 5: Anxiety. There are many synonyms for "anxiety": "worry," "stress," "angst," "tension," "discomfort," "malaise." Whatever you call it, anxiety has been referred to as "the silent killer." It can attack you at any time. It can result from pent-up anger and frustration or prolonged guilt and fear. Any combination of these feelings can produce anxiety that, if left unchecked, can hurt you physically and emotionally.

How do you keep your anxiety in check? By learning to put things in their proper perspective. This is easier said than done, of course, but it's a skill you can cultivate. It requires, however, persistent and daily application until it becomes second nature to you.

What are some common causes of anxiety?

- Trying something new.
- Facing the unknown.

- Overcommitting yourself.
- Expecting the worst most or all of the time.
- Making tough decisions.

Have you ever had to make a really tough decision — one so difficult you found yourself wishing someone else would make it for you? Did you just feel like crawling into some hole and hibernating until it was all over? We all face such challenging decisions, usually on a daily basis. And these decisions influence the directions we take in our lives and the ultimate results we achieve.

We start out each day by making minor decisions, such as which clothes to wear, what to eat for breakfast, or what radio station to listen to (that one can be tough!). We then go to work, where we must decide which strategies to pursue with our clients, which proposals are best, how to talk to the boss, whether or not we should complain about a problem, or when the appropriate time would be to ask for a raise or a promotion. Debating what to do in each situation is stressful enough. Then, once you make a decision, you agonize over it and its possible consequences.

Which college? If you are the parent of a teenager who will soon be heading off to college, you'll relate to the following story. As a senior in high school, I was trying to decide which college to attend. For me, the choice depended on many factors: Which schools accepted me, how much financial aid they offered, and what each of them offered in the way of academic programs, sports, and culture. As it turned out, I was accepted into Georgetown University. Georgetown had a premier language program, and Washington, D.C. seemed to be an ideal place to study government and eventually pursue a political career.

A few weeks later, however, Boston University offered me a full scholarship. When my dad heard the news, he shouted, "Go to BU! Go to BU!" Visions of a debt-free four years were dancing before his eyes. I stopped him, though, and said, "But I want to go to Georgetown!" It was difficult for me to decide between a full-scholarship ride to BU and my ideal university where I could fulfill my passion of studying languages and government and pursue my desire to venture out on my own in a new city. The easy way out would have been to go to BU — but I really wanted to go to Georgetown.

So I sat down with my parents and explained to them how important it was for me to go away to college and become independent. I knew it would be a sacrifice for them, and I knew it would be scary for me, but I felt it would take me closer to where I wanted to go in life. And it did.

Deciding where to go to college is usually very stressful. It's one of the first big steps many people take toward full independence from their families. But you'll make **many** important decisions in your life, one after the other, day after day. Sometimes you'll be proud of your decisions. Other times you'll wish you had taken another route. The important thing is that you keep making choices. The more you do, the less stressful making choices will become.

The worst type of anxiety. Some forms of anxiety are good and even healthy. The anxiety you feel right before giving a speech, for instance, can jump-start your positive adrenaline. The anxiety you feel before asking someone out on a date means you really care about that person and want him or her to say "Yes!"

The worst type of anxiety we can ever experience, I believe, is "fear of the unknown." When you dread the possible outcome of a situation, or belabor the pros and cons of acting because you don't know what the result will be, you end up shortchanging yourself by denying yourself opportunities to grow and succeed. You then end up wasting valuable time and energy that could be better spent pursuing your goals and attending to your needs.

On Tuesday morning, September 11, 2001, life as we once knew it changed dramatically in America. The twin towers of New York City's World Trade Center — formerly a prominent symbol of America's financial prosperity — were destroyed by hijacked commercial airliners. That same morning, the Pentagon — home of our country's military defense and intelligence operations — was also attacked by a hijacked commercial airliner, killing innocent civilians and military personnel. And in Pennsylvania, a third hijacked airliner crashed in the countryside; investigators today believe that plane, too, was heading for Washington, D.C., but that it went down when several heroic passengers figured out what was going on and attacked their assailants.

The death toll from that tragic day rose to nearly 2,800 people. It was the worst assault on American soil since the Japanese had bombed Pearl Harbor in December, 1941.

Part of the "emotional fallout" of this national tragedy has been an uneasy feeling about the future. Some common sentiments: "What will happen in the near future? When will I feel safe again? How can I restore a sense of normalcy to my life?"

We can never predict with certainty what the future will hold. The best antidote for anxiety about the unknown is to focus on the present moment.

Do what you can **today** to be as productive, helpful, and loving as you possibly can. As the saying goes, "You're here today, gone tomorrow." When you practice limiting your concerns to what needs to be done this very day, you'll greatly reduce the number of worries and problems you experience.

Strategies for Overcoming Anxiety and Stress

- Acknowledge your anxiety and determine what external and internal factors are causing it.
- Realize the adverse effect anxiety is having on your life (e.g., sleeplessness, headaches, indigestion, ulcers, chest pain).
- Consider the benefits of a peaceful existence.
- Change your pattern. Slow down if you're getting "burned out." Or, get busy if you've been lethargic and sedentary for too long.

DON'T REINVENT THE WHEEL — REINVENT YOURSELF!

Successful people **must** reinvent themselves many times to achieve their dreams. You can do it, too!

To reinvent yourself, however, you must determine who you want to become and then take steps to get yourself there. It may take a while to develop yourself and grow into your new role, but eventually you'll become a master of your new role in life. Why? Because **you** will have decided to make it a reality. **You** will have decided to pursue another side of yourself, one that had been undeveloped or hidden before. The ability to reinvent yourself is a powerful tool for success and a phenomenal motivator, not to mention a great confidence builder!

Suppose, for instance, that you want to become known as an author but you've never written a book before. Develop some ideas and start writing down your thoughts on paper. Soon, words become sentences … which become paragraphs … which become pages … which become chapters. Before you know it, you've written a book — your own personal masterpiece. People start referring to you as an author. And then you realize that **you** have reinvented yourself! **You** have taken control of your own destiny! **You** have decided to make it happen!

Soon after graduating from college, I decided I wanted to become a motivational speaker. I was inspired by one motivational speaker in particular — Les Brown, author of *Live Your Dreams* (William Morrow and Co., 1993). Brown's philosophy profoundly affected my life. I was drawn to his message that, no matter what circumstances you might face, and no matter what obstacles life throws your way, you can overcome them.

One time a few years back, I was fortunate enough to be able to hear Brown speak in person. I sat in the second row of a seminar he gave in Washington, D.C. He told everyone present that night, "Whatever caused you to be here, don't lose that." That statement caused me to think about why I had decided to attend the seminar in the first place.

I wanted inspiration. I wanted to be reminded of all the potential I had deep inside of me. I wanted to be reassured that the troubling waters I was treading at the time did not signify a dead end for me. I had the power to change my life!

After the seminar I went up to Les, gave him a bear hug, and told him, "You're an inspiration!" I was so moved by his message that I decided I wanted to have the same kind of influence on people's lives. I wanted to touch people's hearts, to motivate them to achieve the greatness they were capable of, and to raise their level of self-awareness.

I dreamed of being a motivational speaker, and of what it would feel like to have an incredible impact on an audience, to be able to move people to action. I wrote down my goal often after that. I soon took a course in public speaking. Then I joined Toastmasters International, a group that gave me the opportunity to do what I dreamed of doing: Speaking before groups of people and sharing inspirational messages with them. Before long, people began to refer to me as a powerful, inspiring speaker. My dream had begun to materialize — because I had taken steps to start making it happen!

POINTS TO REMEMBER

- Discover the source of your greatness.
- Learn continuously.
- Examine your strengths and weaknesses.
- Eliminate the "demons" in your life: guilt, anger, fear, frustration, and anxiety.
- Determine who you want to become, and then take the steps to get there.

THREE

CREATE

Turn Ideas Into Action

"The secret of getting ahead is getting started."

— SALLY BERGER

Sometimes, no matter how optimistic you are, you might feel your life is going nowhere in a hurry. Despite your eagerness to succeed and improve in different areas of your life, you may find yourself unable to break through whatever it is that's holding you back from achieving your goals and fulfilling your dreams.

When you are "stuck," it's important to overcome the roadblocks you face by **Creating** the conditions that will ultimately lead to your success. I'm sure you've heard the expression, "If you don't see a bridge, then build it." Instead of spending your precious time analyzing the problems and obstacles in your path, you can channel your energy toward finding **solutions**. When you change your focus from what's wrong or "not quite right" to what you can **do** to improve your situation, you'll start coming up with ways to do just that.

A CALL TO ACTION

Now that you've spent some time reading and working through the exercises in chapters 1 and 2, you've set some exciting, challenging, and worthwhile goals for yourself. You've also told others about your plans. Now it's time to turn your ideas into action!

Ask yourself, "What's the very first thing I can do to get started?" Maybe you can make a phone call or send an e-mail … or fill out an application … or buy the equipment you need. Learn as much as you can about your subject of interest, and then — whatever you do — get started! Les Brown, author of *Live Your Dreams* (William Morrow and Co., 1993), says, "You don't have to be great to get started, but you have to get started to be great!" Ancient Chinese philosopher Lao Tzu put it this way: "The journey of a thousand miles begins with the first step." These statements capture the true meaning of greatness. All you have to do is take that first step … then another … then another. Before you know it, you will have made progress by great leaps and bounds.

When I decided I wanted to run in a marathon — and that I would finally make this dream a reality — I registered for the race and bought a sturdy pair of running shoes. Then I started running, keeping a log of my workouts and documenting the progress I was making. Small, simple steps helped me put my goal into action. Next, I read some books on marathon training and conditioning. I also received all kinds of advice from people who had run marathons themselves: "Find a plan and stick to it." "Join a running group." "Make sure you cross-train." "Control your breathing." I attended a class as well — "You Can Run a Marathon!" — in which a longtime runner gave practical, helpful advice for long-distance training.

I eventually succeeded in completing a marathon (and then another as well) because I decided to stop making excuses and start taking action. Magical things happen when you resolve to "activate" your life. When you commit yourself to a goal, people seem to come out of the woodwork to help you. Where were these people before? Probably waiting for you to take that important first step!

"The only limit to our realization of tomorrow will be our doubts of today. Let us move forward strong in active faith."
— FRANKLIN D. ROOSEVELT

LET YOUR ACTIONS DO THE TALKING

Goal setting and self-awareness, while necessary for your success, are merely "prerequisites" to prepare you for the starting line on the road to achieving your goals. The next and most critical step is to take **action**! It's never too late to get started on your dreams. Take, for example, George Dawson, whose autobiography, *Life Is So Good* (Random House, 2000), has inspired thousands of people to get up and do something to make their dreams come true — instead of just thinking or talking about them. After nearly 10 decades of being illiterate, Dawson decided it was time to learn how to read. For so many years he had concealed his inability to decipher the written word. So at the age of 100, he started taking classes to educate himself on basic reading and writing skills. Now, at the dawn of his eleventh decade on earth, he can make sense of what used to be merely jumbled symbols on a page.

We can learn a lot from George Dawson's tenacity and boldness in starting something new, even after so many years of missed opportunities. Take a page from Dawson's book: Let your actions — not just your words — do the talking. Here are five ways to do just that:

Use the Resources You Already Have

History shows us that the most productive, effective people are those who realize what they have, appreciate it, and make the best of it. Our 26th president, Theodore Roosevelt, once advised, "Do what you can, with what you have, where you are." When you think about it, what more can you do? Take what life gives you and do the best you can with it.

Whenever you're starting out on a brand new adventure or career path, resourcefulness will be your No. 1 ally in pursuing your vision. Nancy Brinker, founder of the Susan G. Komen Breast Cancer Foundation (www.komen.org) in Dallas, began a mission in 1982 to raise awareness of, and eventually find a cure for, breast cancer.

While Nancy is a survivor of breast cancer herself, her older sister, Susan, was not as fortunate: After a three-year battle with the disease, Susan G. Komen lost her life to breast cancer. Before she died, Susan asked Nancy to promise her to do everything in her power to make sure that other women would not suffer the same fate. Determined to do something to end this deadly disease, Nancy formed a foundation whose mission is to "eradicate breast cancer as a life-threatening disease by advancing research, education, screening, and treatment."

When Nancy first started the Komen foundation, all she had was $200 in a shoebox, a handful of business cards, a few volunteers and a vision —

a vision of garnering grassroots, political and financial support from corporations, associations, and individuals from all over the country. Through the Komen Foundation, Nancy started the Komen Race for the Cure®, a five-kilometer race that takes place annually in more than 100 cities around the U.S.

Nancy has received much recognition and praise from the media and private organizations for her commitment to solving a national epidemic. Because of her commitment to her dream, Nancy has excelled as a communicator, leader, and humanitarian. In 1999, she accepted the "Humanitarian of the Year" award from the Republican Women's Leadership Forum in Washington, D.C.

Nancy could have found any number of excuses for putting off the creation of her foundation (i.e., grief, lack of time, "too big a project"). Instead, she chose to rise to the challenge of fulfilling the promise she had made to her sister Susan and dedicating her life to finding a cure for breast cancer. When **you** decide what **your** vision is, you must go after it with the same level of enthusiasm, courage, and commitment that Nancy Brinker has shown in her quest to realize her dream.

"This country was not built by men who relied on somebody else to take care of them. It was built by men who relied on themselves, who dared to shape their own lives, who had enough courage to blaze new trails — enough confidence in themselves to take the necessary risks."

— J. OLLIE EDMUNDS

Tap Your Brain Power

Success in any endeavor requires imagination. So you need to use your creative genius to develop new and innovative ideas, and to formulate fresh plans.

Sit down and brainstorm for ideas that will make your life richer and more meaningful. Ask yourself, "How can I use my talents to stand out from the crowd and make my mark in life?" "What qualities do I possess that others seek?" Let your creativity come alive — try not to pre-judge your own responses as "dumb," "silly," or "unrealistic" — and you'll soon find yourself coming up with lots of great ideas.

Creativity is the mark of the individual, the essence of your uniqueness. We all have our own set of tools to work with. There are so many combinations, so many variations on how we can live our lives. So create an astonishing life for yourself by understanding what works best for you and what you work best at.

I have had the great fortune to meet and befriend an individual by the name of Michelle James. Michelle and I first became acquainted in Toastmasters International. We first got to know each other as members of the Nancy Brinker Toastmasters club in Vienna, Virginia.

Michelle is an entrepreneur who uses her creativity to help others yet make a living at the same time. She's the founder and president of Creations Unlimited, a consulting company in McLean, Virginia. The purpose of her work is to help organizations and individuals find their creative energy and develop strategies for incorporating more of their own creativity into their work. She achieves this goal by (among other things):

- Conducting seminars on how to determine your creative thinking style and then use that information to increase your productivity and effectiveness.
- Teaching people how to use their unique gifts, skills and abilities, and creativity in their work and in their lives.

After participating in one-on-one counseling with Michelle myself, I was particularly struck by her sincerity and compassion in helping people capitalize on what they already know about themselves. I realized that I wasn't coming anywhere near maximizing my own creative potential on the job. While it appeared (on the surface) that I had a good job, I discovered that I was in fact using less than 20 percent of my creativity in my work. Talk about wasted potential! What about the other 80 percent? After just an hour with Michelle, I resolved to myself that I could do so much more — that I could use so many more of my creative abilities than what I was. The only "reasons" I could come up with for continuing my same routine were **habit** and **convenience**. They weren't substantive enough to keep me where I was. I realized I needed to challenge myself more, to explore my creative and expressive side. Only then would I feel fulfilled emotionally and spiritually.

At one point, I asked Michelle about what had made her decide to start her own business, and why this one in particular. Not surprisingly, she replied that there had been no job out there that she felt really fit her. This realization had led to a turning point where she realized she would have to create her own. So she started her own company, and has watched it evolve over time from a traditional consulting business into a more soulful and creative enterprise.

When Michelle first began her business, she believed her role should be to create what her clients wanted, regardless of her own connection to what she was creating. After doing quite a bit of reflecting and soul searching, however, she realized that her role really should be to get in touch with her **own** creativity in supporting her clients. This epiphany transformed her business from one of obligation to one of fun, engaging service.

Michelle considers herself more of a creativity "cultivator" than a consultant because she believes her role is not to teach or consult, but rather to draw forth and elicit the existing indwelling creativity of those she serves. To that end, she uses her own creativity to help others cultivate theirs.

Even to this day, Michelle notes, her business is constantly transforming and evolving. As she grows and changes personally, her business reflects those changes.

When I asked Michelle about the challenges she'd faced in venturing out on a limb and breaking the mold of "tradition," she told me she'd had to initially overcome fear and self-doubt, both of which are only natural when one is trying something new. Michelle also admitted to making a lot of mistakes when she started out. But, she added, she learned an important lesson — that it's OK to make mistakes. She emphasized that with every new experience in life, you're likely to go through periods of insecurity and doubt. But those feelings fade away with time, giving way to confidence and certainty about your career choice.

Michelle also says that there are distinct advantages to having her own business. She has the freedom to think for herself, to put more of herself into her work, and to choose her own creative destiny.

Take the Initiative

Picture a successful person you know. Maybe a member of your family or community comes to mind. Now, picture what he or she typically does every day. Is the person sitting down doing nothing, or is he or she moving about, always involved in some cause or action? One common denominator among successful people is that they're always **doing**.

In many cases, showing initiative means taking matters into your own hands. One evening, for example, while I was working as a concierge, I received a call from one of the guests at about 6:45 p.m. The guest asked me to ship out, via Federal Express, 60 boxes — each weighing about 20 pounds. He told me the boxes needed to arrive the next morning in Los Angeles.

I pointed out, however, that according to Fed Ex rules, all shipments must be submitted by 6 p.m. to guarantee next-day delivery. Then I remembered that there was a Fed Ex drop-off location just two blocks from the hotel, and it was open until 7 p.m. In my mind flowed the words, "The customer comes first." Hmm … I had 15 minutes to transport 1,200 pounds of material to the Fed Ex station.

So I told the guest, "I'll see what I can do!" I then threw off my jacket and found three stewards from the kitchen to help me. They loaded the first 15 boxes (around 300 pounds) onto a cart and rolled it down the hill with the help of a co-worker. The weight on those wheels could have generated the speed of a freight train! On top of that, I was wearing a pair of loafers, which wasn't making things any easier. We were losing precious moments!

Finally, we arrived at the Fed Ex station. Dripping with sweat, I pulled the cart into the small office. A lady looked at me and said, "Sir, we close in seven minutes. We can't ship out that many boxes on such short notice. However, there is a location 15 minutes from here. It closes at 8:30 p.m." It still seemed like a longshot, but I decided to go for it.

I called the banquet manager at the hotel and asked him to bring around the company van so that we could load up the other 45 boxes. I then ran back to the hotel, leaving one of my co-workers at the Fed Ex station with the bell cart we'd just finished wheeling there. We loaded up the rest of the boxes at the hotel, picked up the remaining boxes and rushed over to the closest Fed Ex station. We found the place before it closed. But … When I went inside, I found out that it didn't accept large shipments. The gentleman said, "You'll have to bring them to Dulles Airport. They close at 10:00 p.m." The airport was 40 miles away! Hmm … I'd gone this far. I was going to finish the job!

So off we went on a 40-mile excursion to Dulles Airport. When we arrived, I followed the Fed Ex trucks onto their property. I then drove into the loading station, where I heard a voice say, "Sorry, that's an unauthorized vehicle." I replied, "Sir, I'm with the Hyatt Corporation. I have half a ton of boxes that need to be shipped out tonight." "Right this way," he replied. Just minutes before the 10 p.m. deadline, we unloaded the boxes and helped the Fed Ex employees load them into the distribution area, from which they went onto the plane. Mission accomplished! In this case, taking matters into my own hands — showing initiative — helped me successfully carry out the guest's request. A moment's hesitation would have prevented us from accomplishing a seemingly impossible mission.

Taking the initiative (i.e., quick, thoughtful action) just may make the difference between succeeding and failing.

Find a Cure for the Common Excuse

To make any great progress in life, you must decide to eliminate the word "excuse" from your vocabulary. We can easily come up with a thousand reasons for **not** following through with our ideas and plans. But life is too short to make excuses for putting your goals off until another day, another week, or another year. When you delay taking action, you wind up taking the easy way out! So choose the less-traveled road — the path of personal accountability.

Here's a list of common excuses that prevent us from living up to our potential:

"I'm too old."

"I'm too young."

"I'm not qualified."

"I missed the boat."

"I don't have enough time."

"I've never done that before."

"I'd make a fool of myself."

"I'd probably fail.

Now, here are some cures for the common excuse:

"It's never too late."

"I'm eager to learn"

"I have what it takes"

"My time will come."

"I will make time."

"I love challenges."

"Who cares about what others think?"

"It's worth taking a chance on."

What are some excuses you've used to talk yourself out of doing things you really want to do? What are some possible cures for these excuses?

EXCUSES	*CURES*
______________________	______________________
______________________	______________________
______________________	______________________
______________________	______________________
______________________	______________________

Your attitude and perspective will determine just how far you go in life. If you make a conscious decision to change your attitude from one of helplessness and narrow-mindedness to one of power and possibility, you will see a dramatic difference in your capacity to get things done.

One prime example of someone who doesn't make excuses is Christopher Reeve, the actor who played "Superman" on the big screen. In 1996, Reeve suffered an accident while riding his horse and became paralyzed from the neck down. Reeve decided not to make any excuses for his impaired ability to speak and move, but instead entered vigorous physical rehabilitation. He also launched a massive national campaign to raise money for paralysis research, and he even made a return to television as an actor and producer. He refused to give up on himself. He wouldn't make excuses for his physical condition. And he didn't allow fear of failure to stand in his way. Reeve's remarkable displays of courage and faith have truly made him a national hero — and a Super Man in the eyes of everyone.

Can you think of a time when you made excuses for not doing something you really wanted to do? Perhaps fear of failure prevented you from following through. Or maybe you thought you'd make a fool of yourself.

When I was in high school, for instance, I was rather shy. I would shrink away from raising my hand in class, afraid that I'd sound stupid and that people would laugh at me. In my sophomore year, I thought about participating in the Foreign Language Declamation — an annual tradition at my high school in which students prepare and recite a five-minute speech in a modern foreign language. I spoke very good French after just a year and a half of studying the language. The tradition within our language department was to have students get up on stage and recite poetry or prose in a foreign language. I was going to participate in the event, but at the last minute I backed out. I'd really wanted to display my French-speaking ability, but **fear** held me back — fear of being on stage and forgetting my lines, and fear of losing miserably. I spent the whole rest of the school year regretting my decision to not enter that contest.

During my junior year, however, I decided to go ahead and enter the event. Not only did I do well, I won! It was an amazing experience, standing up there with the spotlight on me and expressing myself in a foreign tongue. I finally got — or, more accurately, pursued — the chance to use my gifts. You must be willing to do the same thing — to take chances and face your fears so that you can experience the joy of self-expression!

Throw Yourself into the Arena of Life

Robert F. Kennedy once said, "Only those who dare to fail greatly can ever achieve greatly." So if you want to reach your potential in life, you must be willing to risk failure. Think about this: Throughout the 200-plus years of American history, we've had only 42 men serve as president of the United States, the highest office in the nation and, arguably, the world. (Note: Grover Cleveland was the 22nd and 24th president.) Hundreds of people have sought this most enviable position of power and prestige, but so few have achieved it. Among those who have run for president and lost, however, many have achieved greatness in several other areas of their lives.

Take, for example, John Glenn, a former U.S. senator from Ohio. In 1962, Glenn became the first human being to orbit the earth. Much later, in 1998, he became the oldest human being to fly in space.

John Glenn is a wonderful example of **integrity**, **courage**, and **persistence** — all critical elements for a successful life. After gaining fame with his flight in 1962, astronaut Glenn set out to become Senator Glenn from Ohio. Much to his dismay, however, the popular and much-loved hero failed in two campaigns for a Senate seat.

Glenn didn't allow these difficulties to deter him for long, though. He ran for the Senate a third time in 1976 and won. He was then re-elected three subsequent times before retiring in 1998 to return to space for NASA experiments on the aging process.

In 1984, Glenn ran for president and lost, incurring huge debts in the process. But he didn't allow his setbacks to set him back for long. In his bid for the presidency, he risked much and lost. Yet, in his space flights and in his campaigns for the Senate, he risked much and won. John Glenn has dared to fail greatly for his entire adult life — and, as a result, he has achieved greatly.

Glenn continued to move forward, no matter what his circumstances. Whether orbiting in space or debating on the Senate floor, he knew the power of "letting his actions do the talking."

"To achieve greatness, you must throw yourself into the arena of life."
— PETER COLWELL

GROW INTO YOUR DREAM

Whether you're planning to start your own business, building the foundation of a budding career, or working to develop a network of personal and professional contacts, you can simplify the process of acting on your goals into three basic steps.

The first step is to pay attention to **detail**. Determine what specific actions you want to take. Brainstorm for things you can do **immediately** and over the **short term** to jumpstart your career and give yourself the knowledge and expertise you need to be successful in that area. Just start writing ideas down as they come to you. Don't worry about whether you'll be able to do everything on the list. Simply let your thoughts flow freely from your mind onto paper. And think **big** as you do this exercise. You're crafting your career; your future. So give it everything you've got!

From your list of perhaps 20 to 30 ideas you've jotted down, plan to take immediate action on at least five of them. When I was visualizing and planning my future professional speaking career, I used this same strategy. I wrote a list of 30 things I could do to move closer to realizing my dream. Among the tasks on my list were reading certain books and articles, taking courses related to the professional speaking field, and attending seminars on developing and marketing my topic. I completed some of the items in a matter of days. Others would take months to accomplish. But completing my short-term tasks gave me the momentum and motivation I needed to keep working toward my long-term goals.

As you brainstorm specific ways to take action and gain momentum toward your goals, be sure to put a **time frame** around each task on your list. Maybe there's a seminar **next month** on how to start your own business. Maybe your birthday is **around the corner** and Amazon.com has a great discount on a book related to your field of interest. When does the mall close **tonight**? Is there still time **today** to buy some business cards? Keep your mind in perpetual "think" mode, and identify the opportunities and resources around you that will help you work toward your goals. Once you've filled your calendar with seminars, courses, and self-learning experiences, you'll find yourself moving dramatically closer to your destination.

BUILD YOUR DREAM ON A FOUNDATION OF GOALS

When is a good time to start pursuing your dreams? Whether your goal is to achieve financial freedom, buy a home, find more leisure in your life, land the ideal job, start a family, or be self-employed, the best time to start is **right now**!

Start today on building the foundation for your long-term goals. Just as an architect would draft detailed sketches of his or her plans, figure out what your dream is going to look and feel like. Determine how it will fit into the overall scheme of your life.

A Fateful Night of Goal Setting

One evening a few years ago, I was riding the train north to Boston to visit my parents. After reading for a while, I decided to write down some personal goals for the upcoming months and for the next few years. I had six hours to kill, and sleeping on those trains isn't always easy.

So I started writing down some ideas, one of them being to improve my public speaking skills. I figured that doing so would help me in many areas of my life, and that it would be a great way to build confidence in myself. "Within one year, " I said to myself, "I will take a public speaking course." Four months later, I enrolled in a 12-week Dale Carnegie course to improve my communication and interpersonal skills. Knowing this course could really help me communicate better, I was willing to pay the $1,500 tuition to attend the training. Somehow, I managed to scrape together the money just in time, and I enrolled as one of the youngest people in the class.

During the ensuing weeks, I showed gradual improvement in my ability to handle the worry and stress related to speaking in front of an audience, and I developed the confidence to be myself in front of a group of people. The change didn't happen overnight, but by week 12 (graduation night), my close friends had seen a noticeable improvement in my overall attitude and self-confidence.

Wanting to maintain my enthusiasm for public speaking and to continue to improve my skills, I joined a Toastmasters Club. Within four months, I had given 10 speeches and was accelerating through the group's educational program.

What happened to me that night on the train to Boston? I realized the power of writing down precise goals, well-defined time frames for achieving them, and specific reasons why those goals are important to me. Setting those goals helped me achieve my vision of becoming an excellent speaker.

Without Deadlines, You Probably Won't Act

In the situation described above, I not only decided what goal I wanted to achieve, but I also put a timetable on it. This is a universal law of goal setting: **Always give yourself a deadline for achieving your goal**. Even if you have to modify your deadline due to unforeseen circumstances, you still need to start with a specific time frame in mind.

One December night, shortly after my uncle's sudden death, I decided I wanted to become certified in cardiopulmonary resuscitation (CPR). I had received some training in CPR several years earlier but I hadn't been certified. I figured it would be worthwhile to have the knowledge and skill in case an emergency situation were to arise in the future.

But I never put a timetable on this particular goal. I just said to myself, "I'd like to take that course sometime." I didn't even write the goal down. A few years went by, and I eventually remembered that I'd set a goal of becoming certified in CPR but had never done anything about it. So I decided to do something about it. I wrote down, as one of my goals, to finally obtain certification.

Months went by … and I'd still taken no action on the goal! Why did I keep putting it off? It wasn't an incredibly difficult task: All I had to do was pick up the phone, call the American Red Cross, find out when CPR training courses were scheduled, and sign up. No rocket science there!

"What Happened to My Goal?"

Have you ever asked yourself, "What happened to my goal?" Maybe you wanted to be a trapeze artist when you were younger but you never pursued that dream. Or perhaps you've always wanted to be a ballroom dancer but you've never taken any action to start working toward that goal.

Each of us plays the "what if?" game at some point in our lives: "What if I'd become an astronaut?" "What if I'd gone to college and studied my passion?" "What if I'd asked him/her out? He/she might not be married to **her/him**! He/she might be married to **me**!" We all have a few "what ifs" packed away in our closets. Most times we allow our dreams to collect dust and sit idle. When we do, we allow a part of ourselves to die a slow, lingering death. So I encourage you to dig way back in your closet, blow the dust off of your dreams, and pursue them passionately!

Leonardo da Vinci once said, "Iron rusts from disuse; Stagnant water loses its purity and in cold weather becomes frozen; Even so does inaction sap the vigor of the mind." Don't allow inaction to sap the vigor of your mind. Don't allow your goals to become rusty or frozen. Invigorate your mind, body, and soul by taking action on your dreams.

Think about 5 goals you have, "large" or "small," that have been collecting dust. Promise yourself that you'll **take action** on each of them. Choose goals that have been on your mental "to do" list for a long time. Include those that have just recently begun to blossom as a result of new circumstances in your life. Commit yourself to achieving at least three of the goals in the next six months. Write down the first thing you can do to get started on each of them right away:

GOAL	*DEADLINE*	*ACTION*
______	______	______
______	______	______
______	______	______
______	______	______
______	______	______

I had started to wonder why my CPR certification goal had been continuing to elude me for so long. Then, a light bulb flashed in my head one day, and I realized that I hadn't given myself a deadline for achieving the goal. Shame on me! Whenever you don't put a deadline on a goal, other areas of your life become priorities.

"OK," I told myself, "time to hunker down and make this a priority or I won't ever get it done!" It was December 1997, four years after the goal had originated. I wrote down the following phrase: "Get certified in CPR by the end of next year, 1998." Well, at the end of 1998, I had signed up for a CPR course a few days before New Year's Eve. **Yes**! The long-put-off goal would be achieved … or so I thought. I had called too late. The class was booked, but another course would be held in January. Ah, well — I wouldn't achieve the goal **quite** on time, but you can bet that, at this point, it was on my "Top 3 List of Things To Do." I wouldn't let a little setback like a full class prevent me from following through.

I finally took the CPR class the first week in February. I was probably more proud than most when I received my little certification card.

The drawn-out process I've just described taught me a valuable lesson about goal setting: If you want to achieve your goals, you must clearly define — in writing — what it is that you want to achieve, and then give yourself a deadline for achieving it.

"Yesterday is history.
Tomorrow is mystery. Today is a gift.
That is why they call it the present."
— ANONYMOUS

ACCEPT THE INEVITABILITY OF CHANGE

There is one phenomenon that can become either an obstacle or an opportunity for you on the way toward your destiny. It's an occurrence that neither kings nor heads of state are immune to: **change**.

My definition of change is, "A force of nature that propels you from one circumstance to another." Can you think of some common examples of change that take place all around us? If you look up at the sky on a clear night, for instance, you'll notice the changing phases of the moon over the course of a month. If you walk out onto a seashore, you'll find the tide moving in or flowing out at any given moment. And every other year in November, we have the opportunity to elect new political leaders in our local, state, and national governments.

Most people would agree that change is good and even refreshing. Sometimes, though, we experience change against our will. A tragedy occurs that turns our lives upside down and inside out. Or, the opposite occurs — good fortune drops on our laps (e.g., winning the lottery or receiving an inheritance).

We can't control all of the changes in our lives, nor can we control other people's actions. But we can control how we **respond** to changes. You, for example, can decide to become a **victim** of change or a **beneficiary** of change. Which would you typically choose? The answer may seem obvious: "Of course I want to **benefit** from change; I don't want to become a victim!" Why is it, then, that so many people become paralyzed and victimized by change, especially change of the negative variety?

The central idea of this chapter is the importance of taking action to achieve the things you want in life. Action is often the missing ingredient in people's lives, robbing people of the results they're looking for. Daydreaming and wishing for something are clearly not enough. Goal setting and self-awareness (the themes of chapters 1 and 2) are crucial starting points in preparing for greatness, but **nothing great can be achieved without action.** I'll repeat that: **Nothing great can be achieved without action.**

You might be saying to yourself, "All of this talk about taking action sounds good … but, well, I just can't seem to get out of my rut. Things just aren't going my way." Have you ever felt "stuck," or like you were moving but in the wrong direction? Believe it or not, there are ways to get out of that situation. Thousands of people before you have done it, and you can, too.

How to Get Yourself Unstuck

When you find yourself in a mental or an emotional rut, your problems may seem insurmountable. Roadblocks might appear to be everywhere, and you may see your dreams as more out of reach than ever.

We all have the ability to get ourselves out of a rut. So why do you think some people stay in a rut while others are able to leap out of it and make something of themselves? The difference between people who continue to flounder and those who bounce back is that the people in the latter group recognize they can jumpstart their lives again only through **action**. Here's a simple, but winning formula for creating positive, lasting change in your life:

ACTION + BELIEF = CHANGE

Action is the greatest catalyst for change, which in turn is the one constant in our lives that is not only healthy and productive, but also necessary. As a society, we crave change. We don't listen to the same music all the time, for instance. Most musical groups in the Top 10 today won't be there a year from now. Our tastes and attitudes evolve over time, as do our expectations.

Change is a powerful agent of personal growth. Can you imagine doing the same thing every day? driving down the same road? having the same job in the same setting with the same people for 50 years? never trying a new food? never moving to a new city? never taking a risk?

When we develop the courage to **Act** upon our **Beliefs**, we create positive **Change** in our lives. How many times have fear and doubt hindered you from making a positive change in your life? Our beliefs serve as the very foundation on which we build our lives. They determine our attitudes, our thoughts, our relationships with others, and, ultimately, our outcomes.

Now, what happens when we don't act upon our beliefs? We remain exactly where we started. We don't come close to achieving our goals. Essentially, we set ourselves up for disappointment, because the greatest failure comes not from trying and losing, but from not even daring to try. We're thus left with a formula for failure:

REACTION + DOUBT = STATUS QUO

When we combine the "wait and see" approach with hesitation, fear, and procrastination, we find ourselves dissatisfied with life.

One of my favorite metaphors for creating change in my own life is to "get the ball rolling." This phrase brings to mind the image of a gigantic ball that is very heavy and stuck in one spot. The ball represents our **plans**, **ideas**, **goals**, and **dreams**. It takes considerable effort to push and prod the ball to get it rolling. You may even need some help from other people to get it going. But once you do, the ball (your plans, ideas, goals, and dreams) picks up momentum and propels you toward your destination. You quickly find that you're no longer "stuck in a rut." Instead, you're now steamrolling your way to your goals.

Decisive action can put an end to months or even years of procrastination. What does this mean for you and me? In the words of George Eliot, "It's never too late to be what you might have been." One simple action can start a chain reaction of events that ultimately improve your life forever!

Why, then, are so many people afraid of change? More accurately, why are people threatened by it? There are lots of possible reasons. People who fear change may:

- Lack control over their circumstances (or at least feel they lack control).
- Fear the unknown.
- Fear the stress that change typically causes.

For months, I had thought about getting a new job — one that rewarded me for my skills, recognized me for my talents, and compensated me for my efforts. I was stuck in a job with no chance of upward mobility. I had reached a dead end, **financially** and **professionally**. But for some reason, I was afraid to search for something new — something that would give me the opportunity to truly grow. I found myself parked at a dead end road and out of gas. (Don't you hate it when that happens?) Fear and procrastination were preventing me from turning around, revving my engine, and cruising to a better destination.

Finally one day, I realized that simply waiting for things to get better would not solve my problem. I had to do something. So I mustered the courage to pick up the phone during lunch and call a headhunter. That phone call led to an interview the very next day. Within a week, I had found a higher-paying job with better benefits. I had suddenly gone from a virtual dead end … to cruise control!

FROM BASHFULNESS TO BOLDNESS

During my travels as a Toastmaster, I have encountered a remarkable person with great speaking talent — a person who overcame many obstacles to become Toastmasters' 1999 World Champion of Public Speaking: Craig Valentine.

Craig grew up with a speech impediment. At an early age, an older man told Craig that he sounded a lot like Daffy Duck. After being labeled that way, Craig spent years inside a shell — a shell he created to protect himself.

Eventually, Craig got tired of living in that self-created shell. He made a promise to himself that he would turn his situation around. And did he ever turn his situation around! He ultimately became one of the finest communicators in the world. In August 1999, on a stage in front of over 2,000 eager listeners, Craig became the World Champion of Public Speaking for Toastmasters International. It was an achievement that meant more to Craig than simply receiving a nice trophy and special recognition. Craig had proven to himself that his setbacks were only temporary, and that his gift as a speaker was permanent! His vision of speaking greatness had become crystal-clear reality.

One of the resounding themes in Craig's motivational speeches is that "in order to change your life, you must change your mind." Craig changed his mind so that he could transform helplessness to hope, humiliation to happiness, and bashfulness to boldness!

POINTS TO REMEMBER

- Let your actions do the talking.
- Find a cure for the common excuse.
- Grow into your dream.
- Build your dream on a foundation of goals.
- Accept the inevitability of change.

FOUR

CONDITION

Get Ready for Greatness

"I will prepare and someday my chance will come."

— ABRAHAM LINCOLN

We often look at ourselves from two perspectives: Where we are at the present in our lives and where we wish to be in the future. More often than not, there's an inordinately large gap between these two points. If your goal is to shed 40 pounds, for example, there's an obvious difference between what you see in the mirror now and the image of the person you want to become. If your intent is to be a millionaire and lead a quiet, relaxed lifestyle, yet you're thousands of dollars in debt and living from paycheck to paycheck, the disparity between your current situation and the reality you hope to create becomes quite evident. If you're the argumentative type who frequently lashes out at everyone in sight, yet you want to become a more compassionate and understanding person, there's no question that the road toward empathy could be a long, uphill one.

So the question you must ask yourself is, "What will it take to get me from my current circumstances to my ideal circumstances?" The answer: **Conditioning**. We all must condition our bodies for physical greatness, our minds for mental mastery, and our emotions for greater self-control and self-acceptance.

SET YOURSELF UP FOR SUCCESS

Success in almost any area of your life is impossible without adequate mental preparation. Knowing your stuff ... anticipating situations ... being ready, alert, and on your feet — all are critical factors when it comes to pursuing success. Picture the minor league baseball player who has been working on his game in the farm leagues for several years, improving his skills so that he'll be ready if and when the moment arrives when he's called up to the majors. Imagine the perennial pageant contestant, vying for a chance to become Miss America: She may spend years perfecting her skills — such as vocal communication, poise, dexterity, and grace — hoping against hope that her opportunity in the spotlight will come. By mentally preparing for your pursuits through hard work, skill mastery, and self-discipline, you give yourself the best possible opportunity to succeed.

"Change is chance, which favors the mind that is prepared."
— LOUIS PASTEUR

Everyone from athletes to lawyers can tell you how important it is to be mentally prepared if you want to be at the top of your game. Mental preparation boosts your confidence by helping you see that you'll be effective in even the toughest situations. It also:

- Gives you a competitive edge.
- Helps you think on your feet and expect the unexpected.
- Minimizes the anxiety you might feel due to lack of preparation.

It's no wonder, then, that the worldwide organization of the Boy Scouts embraces as its motto, "Be Prepared!" Lord Robert Baden Powell, the man responsible for bringing Scouting to the United States from England and the founder of the Boy Scouts of America in 1910, was once asked by a gentleman, "Be prepared for what?" "Well," he replied, "any old thing!" The motto the Boy Scouts adopted comes from the ancient Code of Knights:

> "**Be always ready** with your armor on, except when you are taking your rest at night. Defend the poor, and help them that cannot defend themselves. Do nothing to hurt or offend anyone else. **Be prepared** to fight in the defense of your country. At whatever you are working, try to win honor and a name for honesty. Never

> break your promise. Maintain the honor of your country with your life. Rather die honestly than live shamelessly. Chivalry requireth that you should be trained to perform the most laborious and humble offices with cheerfulness and grace; and to do good unto others."

I spent the greater part of my childhood and teenage years in the Boy Scouts. From a very young age, Scouting instilled in me the value of preparedness for life's unexpected situations. Scouting taught me what to do if you become stranded in the wilderness and have to make do for shelter, food, and warmth. It also taught me how to respond to emergency situations. Understanding — ahead of time — what you should do (i.e., being mentally prepared) in these scenarios goes a long way toward improving your chances of successfully handling them.

On Christmas Eve of my freshman year in college, I was alone at home while my family was out doing last-minute Christmas shopping. My grandfather, Baba, called me to say that his brother Alfred had fallen down. Alfred, my granduncle and lifelong mentor, was 83 years old, so it was probable that he had just fainted. But when I rushed down to their home, I found him lying on his stomach with a discolored face. I could have panicked, but I didn't; instead, I turned him on his back, called the ambulance, and performed rescue breathing. I did everything in my power to breathe life back into him, but I was unable to revive him.

The ambulance crew arrived shortly thereafter. After several attempts on their part, they gave up. My granduncle didn't make it that night, but I took comfort in the fact that I had remained calm under horrifying circumstances and taken action. Although it had been too late to save him, I know I did everything I could that night, and that I had been ready, willing, and able to help.

Being mentally prepared will not insulate you from failure and disappointments, but it will give you the tools you need to succeed when opportunities arise. As our 16th president, Abraham Lincoln, once said, "I will prepare and someday my chance will come." Lincoln is perhaps the ultimate example of **persistence**, **overcoming setbacks**, an **iron resolve**, and **mental preparation**. Each failure he endured in his life — from a losing early run for the state legislature, to the loss of his sweetheart Ann Rutledge in his late twenties, to his defeats in races for the U.S. House of Representatives and the U.S. Senate — contributed to victory in his run for the highest and noblest office in the land: President of the United States. Certainly, a lack of focus or a weakened spirit would have prevented Lincoln from achieving his ultimate success. But he didn't stop until he was victorious; each setback allowed him to be better prepared for his next venture.

Can you think of a time when you were well prepared to step up to the plate … a time when you had to overcome the disappointment of rejection or defeat, but you continued to work on your skills in preparation for your opportunity … a time when you persevered despite apparent signs of defeat? Write a brief summary of that scenario here:

____

____

____

____

____

____

____

____

____

Reminding yourself about how you overcame previous disappointments will give you the strength to confront future challenges.

Dare to Prepare

Preparing for success is risky business: There's no guarantee as to the outcome of your efforts. The one thing you can count on, though, is the fact that if you don't prepare, you won't succeed. So it is in your best interest to put forth every effort to prepare for the greatness you **know** you're destined for.

Get Ready to Speak Up

Great communicators are like celestial comets: They blaze a trail of light and magnificence everywhere they go, leaving a positive and permanent impression on those they've touched. Can you think of people who have/had extraordinary communication skills? These individuals have the ability to persuade others to take certain actions. They stir the hearts and minds of their listeners. They paint an indelible picture in history, and even after they're gone they remain among the immortals of the world who had a story to tell and told it well.

Words that move mountains. In 1987, President Ronald Reagan — known to many as The Great Communicator — exhorted Soviet leader Mikhail Gorbachev with these powerful, commanding words: "Mr. Gorbachev, **tear down this wall**!" As a result of Reagan's message, the Berlin Wall — which had divided East and West Germany for three decades — came tumbling down, and with it the wall of communism.

In 1963, Dr. Martin Luther King, Jr., told a throng of supporters and the American people as a whole, "I have a dream … ." He regaled us with his vision of racial equality, greater acceptance, and personal freedom. King's speech didn't come from a sheet of paper; it reverberated from his soul. It sang from his heart and echoed from the depths of his being. His passion and commitment to his cause made him an effective communicator. His message that day was crystal clear to everyone who heard it.

President Franklin Delano Roosevelt told a nation of unemployed and desperate people during the Great Depression, "The only thing we have to fear is fear itself." FDR's message came at a time when one-third of the people in the country had no job, little money, and vanishing hopes. Fear was more abundant than ever — fear of not being able to provide for one's family, and fear of being poor and dying of hunger. Roosevelt soothed the country's aching heart by giving Americans courage and hope.

Here are just a few of the many benefits you'll reap from mastering communication skills:

- Stronger rapport with friends and associates.
- Better understanding by others.
- Improved self-confidence.
- Greater ability to sell people on your ideas and projects.

The ability to communicate well is one of the most critical tools you need to create successful and lasting relationships with others, personally and professionally. Effective communication is the basis of effective leadership. It's the engine that fuels your ability to get along with people, forge alliances, mediate disagreements, and negotiate your views with those who hold different opinions.

Get Ready to Listen Up

Of all aspects of communication, the most effective — and most overlooked — is the ability to **listen** well. When most people think of communication, they think of speaking, gesturing, or some other physical form of expression. Listening, conversely, is often viewed as a passive experience. In reality, however, listening is one of the most **active** forms of communication ... if done effectively. When you listen to people, you must give them 100 percent of your attention. You must work hard to understand what they're trying to tell you, to interpret their body language, and to see things from their perspective. You can't do this if you let your mind wander and start thinking about all of the things you have to get done — the tasks you **wish** you were working on instead of listening to your counterpart.

Good listening worked wonders on my first date — a blind date — with my then-future wife. I figured a nice, quiet dinner would be appropriate. It would be a chance for us to relax and get to know each other. Well, we spent three hours at the table getting to know each other. Most of the time, I was eating my spaghetti, giving consistent eye contact and just listening. I resisted the urge to tell Trevia all about myself, my accomplishments, my hopes, my fears. Instead, I let her shine. I uttered no more than a few sentences the whole evening. That night, I found out more about her life in three hours than I knew about most of my friends — simply because I decided to listen. And so the two of us hit it off. She'd found a wonderful listener, and I'd found someone with the gift of gab. What a match!

Listening may well be the most beneficial form of communication. Great leaders listen to people's needs. People who do the best in sales and marketing listen to the needs of their clients, not just to their desire to make money and increase profits.

Get Ready to Lead

True leaders share uncommon qualities that set them apart from followers. Leaders are able to articulate a vision, purpose, or mission. Furthermore, they're able to mobilize themselves and others to take action and get things done.

One of the greatest compliments I've ever received came from a woman I collaborated with several times while coordinating a political event. Although I had never met the woman face to face, we had communicated through phone conversations, e-mail, and faxes. One day, she called to tell me that she hoped to be able to meet me one day in person — and that, if she did, she'd shake my hand and thank me for being so efficient, responsive, and productive. She said: "I've never met anyone before who had such an extraordinary ability to get things done. I can't stop singing your praises to my colleagues." Needless to say, her genuine comment made my day!

Another excellent (and less personal!) example of leadership in action is Barbara Brown, a professional speaker and business trainer from Washington, D.C. Barbara started her management consulting and training company in 1993 after a successful 19-year career in the federal government. During her employment, she occupied several management positions in training and human resources, supervising both managerial and non-managerial employees.

Her decision to become an entrepreneur was fueled by nothing more than a desire to "do her own thing." It had nothing to do with lack of career advancement or opportunity. In fact, during her federal government career, she received a promotion every two years, on average. Barbara's choice to start her own business was driven by her personal need to have greater control of her future — both financially and professionally. Although she knew that continued advancement in her current organization was inevitable, her professional growth, freedom, and creativity in the federal government, or in private industry for that matter, was limited by the organization itself. Consequently, for Barbara, taking the entrepreneurial route was part of a personal desire to see what she could accomplish, and to discover what other opportunities existed beyond the confines of a typically structured organization.

Starting her own business was naturally a major turning point in Barbara's life. But most importantly, it was the "best career decision" she ever made. For her, "best career decision" means that she, rather than a corporation, has the greatest influence over her destiny. And there's a certain feeling of accomplishment, satisfaction, and fulfillment she gets from being the decision maker and the benefactor of her efforts.

That doesn't mean she hasn't faced obstacles. She has. For example, her first contract, which was supposed to last for six months, resulted in only two weeks of work. In another instance, her training contract was terminated because a new training director didn't like her. As she points out, being an entrepreneur brings a set of specific challenges. Dealing with rejection, struggling to maintain a steady flow of income, and trying to build credibility are just a few of them.

But along with difficulty comes pleasure. And part of that pleasure involves the satisfaction you feel when you encounter an obstacle and find ways to overcome it. Barbara has dealt with obstacles by relying on the leadership skills that are necessary for success in any business. First, she always keeps the vision of what she wants to achieve — her short- and long-term goals — foremost in her thoughts. That way, she knows where she's going. So when she runs into a roadblock, she uses that vision of her future to energize herself and propel herself forward.

Second, Barbara recognizes the value of establishing and maintaining relationships. Whether through periodic phone calls, a written note to say "hello," or a monthly email newsletter, she keeps her name in front of what she calls the "Three P's" of her client base: **p**ast, **p**resent, and **p**otential customers. That way, when she loses one client, her chances are greater for getting a replacement. In fact, she has had clients contact her after being on her mailing list for four years!

Lastly, Barbara continuously strives to find ways to maximize her performance in both her business operations and her leadership development pursuits. She knew, for example, that if she wanted to succeed in business, she needed to stay self-motivated and self-developed. As such, she became an avid user of books and tapes.

When Barbara first started her business, her primary stockpile included what she called the "Two M's of Performance Management" — **m**otivational topics and **m**arketing topics. Susan Jeffers, Anthony Robbins, Wayne Dyer, and Norman Vincent Peale were her constant companions during those early years. She used their books and tapes as "wake-me-ups" and "pick-me-ups." Her second cache of materials revolved around marketing. Here, Jay Conrad Levinson, author of the *Guerrilla Marketing* books, was her coach. Finally, she became committed to developing into an expert on her topic; she returned to school to learn more about leadership development, read books, attended conferences, and took on leadership roles in associations.

The techniques Barbara has used to overcome obstacles represent her fundamental approach to leadership development, which she describes as **V**isioning, **I**nfluencing, and **P**erforming (V.I.P.). She believes that, to succeed in business, entrepreneurs must know what goals they want to achieve, be able to influence others to help them achieve those goals, and have the capacity to optimize their performance. That's how Barbara has succeeded in business, how she has stayed in business, and how she plans to continue in business.

(Note: Barbara speaks on the universal application and transforming power of **V**isioning, **I**nfluencing, and **P**erforming (V.I.P.) leadership skills. Her recent book is entitled *Becoming a V.I.P. Leader: Transforming Leadership Strategies for Managers and Non-Managers* (Leader Learning, 2002). Visit Barbara's web site at www.aboutbarbarabrown.com.)

As you begin developing your leadership skills, you'll start to see many benefits. Among them:

- More opportunities to advance your career.
- Greater earning potential.

- More opportunities to implement your ideas.
- Ability to influence others positively.

Think of the leaders who have influenced your life by bringing out the best in you, teaching you important lessons about yourself, or broadening your horizons in some way. I, for instance, will long remember a lesson my Scoutmaster taught me when I was 11. Our troop had gone on an all-day hike in the woods. We'd brought our backpacks, food, maps and compasses, first aid kits, knives, and extra clothes. During a lunch break, we sat on some boulders and ate our lunch, whittled, and just relaxed. Then, one of the other Scouts asked to use my knife to whittle. So I handed it to him — open and with the blade facing him.

When we got back from our trip, the Scoutmaster took me aside, looked me in the eyes, and said, "I hate to have to do this, Peter, but I'm going to have to take your Totin' Chip away." I had lost my privilege to carry a knife with me on camping trips. I had violated the rules by incorrectly handing the knife to the other boy. Tears came streaming down my face. I felt ashamed and sad that day, but I learned an important lesson: Never again did I mishandle a knife. I learned to respect knives as potentially harmful weapons, and eventually I earned the right to carry one again. By disciplining me for my behavior, my Scoutmaster not only taught me a valuable lesson, but also showed me that being a good leader means doing the right thing, no matter what.

Being liked vs. being a leader. If you want to be liked by absolutely everyone, you may want to think twice about becoming a leader. Leadership requires you to make decisions that you feel are in the best interests of those you're leading — even if those people ultimately disagree with your actions. A former human relations instructor of mine once told me, "Leadership boils down to care." Those words have been imprinted in my mind ever since. The challenge you face as a leader is to follow your conscience and do what you feel is right, no matter what. When my Scoutmaster took away my right to carry a knife, for example, he knew it wouldn't make him popular. But his duty to do the right thing outweighed his desire to be liked.

Leadership is essential in the workplace, at home with your family, in your other personal relationships, and even in your "inner dealings" with yourself. You must lead your life based upon your **own** values and your **own** conscience. An often missing ingredient in people's leadership styles is **compassion**. Compassion is an outward expression of love that many great leaders demonstrate to their constituents. Most people wouldn't mention love and leadership in the same breath, but the two really do go hand in hand. Genuine love requires courage, commitment, and action. Leadership calls for the same things. Dr. M. Scott Peck summed it up best in his book, *The Road Less Traveled* (Simon & Schuster, 1985):

> "Love is not simply giving; it is judicious giving and judicious withholding as well. It is judicious praising and judicious criticizing. It is judicious arguing, struggling, confronting, urging, pushing, and pulling in addition to comforting. It is leadership."

Almost any situation you'll ever face will require leadership of one sort or another. Decision-making, risk taking, and time management are integral parts of our everyday lives. Continuing to make decisions, take risks, and manage multiple tasks will increase your effectiveness as a leader in everything you do.

There is a leader inside every one of us. Sooner or later, your chance to exert leadership will come. Will you be ready?

"Leadership is the capacity to translate vision into reality."
— WARREN BENNIS

Get Ready to Serve

Being able to interact with various types of people is an ability many people have not fully developed. Most of us aren't born with polished people skills. Fortunately, though, we can develop and master them with practice and an open mind.

How do you handle hostile or arrogant people? Do you blow up in their faces, or do you calmly listen, bite your tongue, and respond maturely and diplomatically? Most people go with their gut instinct: If someone makes them angry, they shout right back at them. What is solved by this sort of response? Nothing! It only heightens the tension and makes matters worse. So learning to deal with conflict and hostility may be one of the most important growth activities you can pursue.

During my days as a hotel concierge, I once had a gentleman (if I must call him that) complain to me that the service in our facility was lousy, that the staff was incompetent, and that his stay with us was the worst hotel experience of his life. Nothing we did to help this man could appease him. In fact, the more we tried to please him, the more irate he became. This man fell under the category of the chronically dissatisfied. Do you know anyone like him? Nothing is ever good enough for them. They're so focused on what's wrong with the world that they fail to see what's right.

Let's just say that this guy put my people/service skills to the test. In the hospitality industry, employees are trained to be attentive to the needs of the guests and to accommodate them in any way possible. In hotels of high caliber, the goal of every staff member is to exceed the expectations of the guests. We had attempted to do just that, but it wasn't enough to satisfy this particular man.

Instead of taking the man's insults personally, however, I asked him: "What can we do to better serve you? Obviously, we haven't met your expectations, and for that I apologize. Is there anything we can do to make it better for you? Please let us know." This approach completely took the wind out of his sails. He didn't have much to say in return, but I did receive an apology from him before the end of his stay.

Occasionally, people you meet will test your patience. Ninety percent of the time, they'll have a legitimate reason to complain. But even if they do not, it's usually best to at least hear them out — and to serve them (or at least try) as best you can.

"In all things, success depends upon previous preparation, and without such preparation there is sure to be failure."
— CONFUCIUS

Some of the most compelling and heroic examples of service emerged on September 11, 2001, when terrorists attacked the World Trade Center in New York City (as well as the Pentagon in Washington, D.C. and a plane that ultimately crashed in Pennsylvania). One example of hundreds: Rick Rescorla, a 62-year-old vice president of corporate security for brokerage firm Morgan Stanley. Rescorla demonstrated rare courage and leadership on that terrible day. Due in large part to his efforts, his firm lost only six of its 2,700 employees in the South Tower. Because he had drawn up evacuation plans for the building in the event of an emergency, Rescorla oversaw the successful exit of nearly all of his company's employees — ultimately losing his own life in the process.

According to a *Washington Post* story written shortly after the tragedy, Rescorla had always been a "model for aspiring leaders" because of his willingness to step into a guiding role and serve others. During battle in Vietnam, he'd been known for singing before the most dangerous battles to make his troops feel at ease. Morgan Stanley employees reported that they could hear Rescorla singing as he directed people out of the tower into safety. As the building fell, he was still looking for those left behind. He didn't survive the building's collapse. But he proved that there are still noble leaders out there who are willing to serve their fellow human beings in times of tremendous need.

ARE YOU READY?

Success depends upon one trait more than any other: **readiness**. Babies, for instance, don't walk or talk until they're ready to do so. While we adults have placed chronological expectations on when infants should start mouthing phrases and sentences, when they should take their first steps, or when they should start using the toilet independently, it is ultimately up to each individual child to decide when he or she is ready.

You can't force another person to succeed until — and unless — he or she is ready to do so. Often, it is simply a question of timing and the person's level of maturity. Take, for example, romantic relationships. Many people just aren't ready for an involved relationship with someone else. A strong, lasting relationship between two people demands — from **both** parties — a high level of commitment to working together and to finding solutions when things go wrong. Relationships also require mutual patience, understanding, responsibility, perseverance, and unconditional love. Not everyone is able, or emotionally ready, to make that type of commitment.

How, then, do you become emotionally ready for a success like marriage? This would be a good question to pose to the 50 percent of married Americans who eventually go through divorce. How do you develop patience? commitment? responsibility? The best way to prepare is to put yourself in "practice" situations. Before making the leap into marriage, for instance, you could test the waters by dating various people and discovering what your relationship strengths and weaknesses are. Dating can become the testing ground where you learn about yourself and how you relate to others.

Even the heartbreak and sorrow from failed relationships can help you expand your self-awareness and decide what your "bottom line" is when it comes to issues of self-respect, commitment, and love. What do you want out of a relationship? What are you looking for in a partner? What aspects of another person's personality can you overlook? Conversely, where do you draw the line with respect to what you'll tolerate?

Moving away from marriage and relationships, suppose your goal is to enter politics or some other form of public service. You can become emotionally prepared for this new role by learning the art of politics. What does it take to succeed in the political arena? What skills do you need to develop? The first one might be public speaking, especially if you're not strong in that area. A politician must be a skilled communicator. So take a public speaking course to improve your presentation abilities. Now, think of what other types of skills you'll need: Human relations … sales and marketing … fundraising. Build your expertise in each of these areas.

Ask yourself the following types of questions:

- What will I have to change about myself before I feel ready to embrace this new lifestyle?
- Who can I model who is already successful doing what I want to do?
- What is the "essence" of this goal? What will my life be like if/when I fulfill this goal?
- What steps can I take now to "get myself ready" to achieve this goal?

I recently met a gentleman at a Toastmasters meeting who works for a distinguished congressman from Texas. The man I got to know is president of another Toastmasters club that meets on Capitol Hill, and he was visiting our club in southwest D.C. After I gave a speech on celebrating our uniqueness, the two of us chatted for a while about our jobs, which both related to government. The man was about six years older than I, and we seemed to have much in common. We were both leaders in Toastmasters clubs. We both saw the value of effective communication skills. We both read books by authors such as Dale Carnegie, Tony Robbins, Les Brown, Stephen Covey, and Warren Bennis. He told me he enjoyed working as a staffer on Capitol Hill, but that he really wanted to run for office himself. So I asked him what his plan was for pursuing that ambitious goal.

I was pleased to hear that he had set a deadline for achieving his goal: He said he could see himself in office in five years. In the meantime, he was taking courses that help prospective political candidates prepare for public office, on topics like handling the media, giving effective "sound bites," employing effective fundraising techniques, and enlisting the support of "power players." Clearly, my new acquaintance had a goal in mind. But he was **also** taking the necessary steps to develop the key skills that would help him reach his goal. I told him, "I have no doubt that you'll be 'the congressman from Texas' in five years." With that kind of unfailing determination and emotional preparation, nothing can stand in his way!

"Preparation ripens the fruit of possibility."
— PETER COLWELL

Some Food for Thought

Here's a great example of being ready in the right place at the right time. One day, while I was working as a legislative assistant at Ernst & Young, I headed to work thinking it was just going to be the typical, usual day. I'd been planning to attend a Brown Bag luncheon, mainly for the **free food**. The luncheon turned out to be a Toastmasters Demonstration Meeting, intended to charter a new club in our company and to "sell" prospective members on the benefits of the program. Although I was already a member of two other Toastmaster clubs in the area, I figured I'd sit through the meeting and then get my **free food**!" So I sat in the last seat of the back row. Soon, we came to the portion of the meeting known as "Table Topics," when someone known as the Topic Master gets up and asks questions of members of the audience, who, if called upon, have to get up and give a one- to two-minute impromptu talk on the subject. Although I considered myself a good speaker, I still get butterflies at the prospect of speaking on a topic without prior preparation.

As I leaned my head down reading through a magazine, the Topic Master said, "That gentleman all the way at the end with his head down." As I looked up, I saw everyone staring at me! "Oh, no!" I thought. "How did this happen to me?" My heart pounding, I approached the front of the audience and read the question addressed to me: "How would you describe yourself in just one word?" Whew! I could answer that one with relative ease. I confidently looked at the audience and said the most fitting word to describe me would be "positive." Then I outlined several reasons to back up my self-assessment.

Toward the end of the meeting, the leaders of the event announced that they were forming a new Toastmasters club in our company. Then, before I knew what was happening, they selected officers and nominated me for president! I gladly accepted and signed the documents acknowledging our newly chartered club. I came for **free food** and left with a leadership position in a brand new organization. Not bad for a day's work!

Timing played a critical role in what happened to me that day. But even more importantly, I had been ready to take on the challenge of starting up a new club, a venture that is exciting and demanding at the same time. If I hadn't been emotionally prepared for such an undertaking — or if I had not developed strong leadership skills beforehand — my presence at the meeting would have meant nothing: I would not have been able to assume the leadership position that was offered to me.

You never know when your chance to shine will appear! It may be just around the corner. Maybe it will reveal itself to you when you're on your way to worship or to attend a meeting. By being emotionally ready and developing communication and leadership skills, you'll be able to take advantage of the "hidden" opportunities that sneak up and surprise you!

It's a Dad Thing

A friend and co-worker of mine once shared with me a very personal story of how she's learned to deal with the loss of her dad.

Pam's story is particularly touching. We can all relate to the tremendous sense of loss and hopelessness we feel after the death of a loved one. Pam and her dad shared an exceptional bond with each other, unlike any other dad and daughter I've ever known. There was just a "special something" between the two of them. They could communicate with each other and know each other's feelings without having to say any words. So when Pam's father passed away on a Halloween night, she felt an emptiness unlike any she'd ever experienced before. An integral part of her life had been taken away from her, instantly. Fortunately, Pam was blessed with love and support from her husband and daughter, as well as her mom and siblings — all of whom helped to see her through the difficult grieving period that followed.

On Christmas morning, the first Christmas without her Dad, Pam sat on the front stairs inside her house, talking on the phone with relatives. While she was chatting, her brother went outside to the mailbox and pulled out an envelope. He then came back in, handed the envelope to Pam, and said, "You got some mail."

Pam looked quickly at the envelope, figuring it was a Publishers Clearing House sweepstakes invitation, and set it aside. Then, she glanced at it again, and opened up the envelope. As it turns out, she was in for a big Christmas surprise! Inside the envelope was a check from her dad — the money he had willed to her in his estate. Pam immediately burst into tears, and she told me she could feel her father with her, gently telling her that even though he was gone, everything was going to be alright.

Then, something suddenly occurred to her: Mail isn't delivered on Christmas Day. The rest of her family didn't receive their checks until well after New Year's Day. This didn't make any sense. **No one gets mail on Christmas Day**! How could she possibly explain what had happened? For her, it was simple: "It's a Dad thing."

Since that unforgettable day, Pam has learned to accept the physical loss of her father, knowing that he's still looking out for her and that, no matter what obstacles she faces in her life, everything is going to be OK.

Think of a time when you suffered a loss. Maybe it was the death of a loved one, the end of a romantic relationship, or even the departure of your child to college and on to adulthood. How did you deal with the loss? Were you able to overcome it and move on with your life? If so, what gave you the strength to keep going? If not, is the pain holding you back from making a fresh start?

You may be wondering why it is so important for you to think about painful experiences from your past. How is that going to help you? You probably want to forget about those terrible times and move on with your life. These are very common — and sensible — questions. The reason it's so critical for you to remember how you've dealt with loss is that it is during our darkest moments in life that we learn some of our most important lessons. We can draw upon these moments to give us the strength and emotional preparation we need to confront new challenges.

Never lose sight of the lessons you've learned from past losses. Everything happens for a reason — to teach us something about ourselves. You can use what you learn to ready yourself for all of the new lessons you'll be learning in the future.

"Those things that hurt, instruct."
— BENJAMIN FRANKLIN

TAKE THE PHYSICAL CHALLENGE

Every human body has its own patterns and reactions to external stimuli. None of us responds exactly the same to certain foods. None of us has the same physiological dynamics as someone else. None of us has the same sleeping, eating, or exercise habits as someone else either. Therefore, all of us need to respect our **own** individual physical needs.

If we let our physical selves go, we show a lack of respect for ourselves. Norman Vincent Peale, in his perennial best-selling book, *The Power of Positive Thinking* (C.R. Gibson Company, 1970), says, "Our physical condition is determined very largely by our emotional condition, and our emotional life is profoundly regulated by our thought life." To say that our thoughts and our physical condition have a strong link would be an understatement. Suppose you carry around with you thoughts of fear, guilt, hopelessness, and incompetence. Do you think you're likely to garner the motivation to start and stick to a fitness plan over a long period of time? Probably not. If you develop a "can do," positive attitude, however … and focus your thoughts on the endless possibilities around you … and remind yourself constantly of the benefits of a healthier, fitter lifestyle, don't you think you're more likely to succeed in your quest for a trimmer body and a stronger cardiovascular system?

Depending on what sport or activity you pursue or want to pursue, get advice from experts in that area on proper training techniques and guidelines. That way you'll set yourself up for success, not disappointment.

The Magical Ingredient – Sleep

There is one "magical ingredient" that is paramount to good physical (not to mention mental and emotional) health. It is one of the few necessities of our lives — something we can't live without. In fact, when we don't get enough of it — as is the case for millions of people around the world — we're not able to function at our optimum levels; we can't be our best.

This magical (but often missing) ingredient has the power to heal your body, refuel your system, and revitalize you. What is it? **Sleep**! Research by the National Sleep Foundation, as reported in *New Choices* magazine in June 1998, found that "sleep-starved workers in this country cost employers as much as $18 billion in lost productivity each year." The study also found that "one driver in three reported falling asleep behind the wheel at least once in the past year."

As this research indicates, not only does an adequate amount of sleep enhance your health and overall productivity, but it can also quite literally save your life.

There are times in our lives when we need more sleep than usual. When a woman is pregnant, for instance, she generally needs more time to rest her body than she otherwise might. If you're undertaking heavy and consistent physical training, your body will need more time to replenish and refuel itself; your muscles must heal and strengthen themselves, so a good 10 to 12 hours of sleep may be in order. Generally, though, eight hours of sleep each night seems to do the trick for most people. Too much sleep can make you sluggish, while too little (a far more common malady in this country) can make the day drag on for you.

Getting enough sleep also improves your short-term memory. Studies have shown that lack of sleep produces forgetfulness and slows down your brain's ability to function at optimum levels.

Can you see the connection between **sleep** and conditioning yourself for **success**? Sleeping is a habit pattern. Some of us have good sleeping habits: We get to bed early and rise early with lots of energy. Most of us, however, fall victim to sleep deprivation: We miss out on valuable rest by working long hours and running ourselves into the ground. So if you really want to get the most out of your working hours, be sure to do your body and mind a favor by getting a sufficient amount of sleep each night.

The 5 Percent Factor

When conditioning yourself for success, you need to incorporate physical training (along with mental and emotional preparation) into your daily life. While it's true that intense sports like marathoning, swimming, and rowing are "95 percent mental," don't underestimate that 5 percent that falls under the physical umbrella. Without it, you won't make it to the finish line of a marathon … or swim that final lap in the pool … or complete those last strokes on the river.

You must, however, give your body enough time to adjust to physical conditioning. Even world-class athletes who train rigorously for months and months occasionally find themselves running out of steam. Bill Rodgers, the world-famous runner and former winner of the Boston Marathon, tells the story about when he had to drop out of his first marathon. Although he had trained extensively and felt well prepared to face the big race, he cramped up with less than 10 miles to go and was forced to bow out of the race.

If you're just starting out and you haven't trained consistently for a long time, you'll face even more demanding physical challenges. Do everything you can to be ready for them by following these four strategies:

Be Consistent

Perhaps the most important element of any fitness program, at any level, is **consistency**. Developing a fitness plan and sticking to it on a regular basis is the best way to ensure your success. Until you develop a daily or weekly exercise ritual, you won't see significant results. The one-day diet never seems to work for some reason, and the now-and-then workout at the gym won't ever get you the results you desire.

I've tried the off-and-on approach to working out. It doesn't work. So commit yourself to exercising reasonably vigorously at least three times a week. Start small, then gradually increase the length, intensity, and frequency of your workouts. It's consistency you're striving for — consistency that will help you get in better shape and stay that way for the long term.

Set Achievable Fitness Goals

Only **you** know what your limits are. So **you** must determine if you can realistically reach your desired level of fitness in a certain time frame. If you want to lose 50 pounds in 5 days, for example, you're setting yourself up for major disappointment. Fifty pounds in five **months** is a bit more achievable, though even that goal will likely be a challenging one.

By all means, set fitness goals that stretch your comfort zone. Just don't stretch yourself until you snap! If you do, your motivation will disappear and you'll end up right back where you started — or at an even worse place.

Challenge Yourself

We are all fueled by a challenge, whether it be physical, mental, or emotional. In fact, I would venture to say that, as a species, we thrive on challenge. When our skills and talents are put to the test, we have the opportunity to surpass even our own expectations.

The only way you'll witness dramatic change in your physical fitness is to push yourself from time to time to reach higher levels. So when you're doing your run/walk, for example, work to increase the amount of time you run and decrease the amount of time you walk. At the age of 62, my mom decided it was time to get herself into great physical shape. So she began by walking 20 minutes a day, and gradually increased the speed of her stride. She then advanced to a regimen of walking **and** running on the treadmill at her local fitness center. After just eight months of consistently challenging herself to do a little more each day, she was up to walking 25 miles a week. Her energy level and vitality have increased dramatically as a result of her commitment to push herself.

The more demanding the goals you set for yourself, the more drive you'll have to move toward your destination.

Eat Healthy

You've probably heard the expression, "You are what you eat, from your head down to your feet." While you may not transform yourself into an egg salad or a hamburger, there is at least a grain of truth to this idea. Studies have shown that the food you digest can affect your moods, alter your behavior, and influence your physical health.

So when you're beginning your exercise program, be prepared to adjust your diet to meet your changing physical needs. If you're doing long-distance running, for example, your body will need more carbohydrates and fiber than usual.

If you don't give your body what it needs from a nutritional standpoint, you will not be able to fully condition yourself for maximum performance and success.

Avoid the Three Os

Many goal-oriented people tend to become "overachievers" — people who go above and beyond in everything they do. While "going the extra mile" is a wonderful trait to have, sometimes you'll need to reduce your activity to avoid ruining your health. So watch out for "the Three Os":

Overtraining

It's very common for beginning and veteran athletes alike to commit the cardinal sin of physical fitness: overtraining. Overtraining can be the result of a zealous attitude, a desire to become totally fit overnight, or even a slightly exaggerated idea of what level you're currently at physically.

Many top athletic coaches recommend exercise programs through which you **gradually** increase your fitness, one sensible step at a time. Your body needs the chance to respond to new stimuli and different routines. So if you start out doing too much too fast, you'll find yourself regretting the almost certain results: Physical pains and/or injuries as well as loss of confidence and motivation.

Whatever physical goal you set out to accomplish, the No. 1 rule is to make it **fun**. Vary your routines. Change the length of your workouts. Go all out one day, then ease through your activities the next. **Enjoy** the process of getting into shape and keeping fit. If you dread doing it — or if you do it because someone else expects you to — you'll be much more likely to slip back into your old routines and habits.

Overeating

Many people can relate to this one. Overeating is often an escape mechanism people use to deal with their troubles.

Your body needs only a certain amount of fats, carbohydrates, and proteins in a given day. The amount varies depending on your height, weight, metabolic rate, and any other physical conditions you may have. If you eat more than your particular body needs, you may suffer a variety of problems ranging from indigestion and vomiting to nausea and illness. Simply reducing the size of your meal portions can help you control excessive weight gain and increase your energy level.

Overworking

Another corporate American phenomenon is the 60- to 80-hour work week. Maybe you bring your work home with you. Or maybe you go to work early and stay late. While many people see nothing wrong with this type of behavior — and some even promote it in a way — it can be harmful in a variety of ways. Among them:

- You lose time with family and friends — time that can never be retrieved.
- Your productivity goes down, as does your energy, while your stress and anxiety invariably go up.

Avoid unnecessary burnout and fatigue by stepping back from your work and making time for other activities and interests.

IT'S ALL IN THE CONDITIONING

If you want to set yourself up for success, **Condition** yourself to think and act like the person you want to become. Preparing mentally for your moment of opportunity will help you perform when it really counts.

As the ancient Asian proverb goes, "When the student is ready, the teacher will appear." To achieve your full potential, you need to realize that there is greatness within you. Give yourself a chance to bring it out by learning to become a better communicator, leader, and servant. And don't forget to take care of your physical health while you're at it; doing so will enable you to meet life's challenges, feel good about yourself, and truly live up to your greatness!

POINTS TO REMEMBER

- Set yourself up for success.
- Get ready to speak up and listen up.
- Get ready to lead.
- Get ready to serve.
- Take the physical challenge.

FIVE

ENVISION

Align your vision and values

"Always keep the sublime objective of your vision in mind."

— MARK FISHER

For centuries, people have tried to focus a "telescope" on the future and see their own fates. Prophets predicted calamity, disasters, and great fortune. They described, in great detail, the rise and fall of peoples and empires. Pioneers foresaw a better existence than their own, and they shared that vision with anyone who would listen.

All of us have the power to develop a picture of the future. You don't need to be a psychic or a mystic; but you do need to **Envision** what you want to do, where you want to be, and when you want to get there. So develop a vision of yourself achieving the greatness you deserve!

THE POWER OF VISUALIZATION

It's a mistake to underestimate the tremendous power of visualization. When you set personal goals, you're essentially visualizing yourself in the near or distant future accomplishing some task or achieving some milestone. Painting a mental picture of yourself doing something you set out to do sends signals to your brain that the achievement is a **possibility** for you.

When I trained for my first marathon, I would frequently conjure up a vision of myself gracefully and effortlessly striding past various points of the race course. After just a few weeks of training — and, mind you, I had never run more than five miles at one time — I was envisioning "Powerful Pete" reaching Mile 20 with relative comfort and ease. I pictured a spirited, focused, and energetic runner who was determined to cross the finish line no matter what. That spirited, focused, energetic runner was **me** — Mr. Peter "I've never run more than a few miles" Colwell was going to achieve these mental and emotional states.

During the summer training months, I'd write down affirmations like, "I **will** run 26.2 miles, with much energy in reserve!" and "I am powerful, confident, and ready to run!"

Then came the day of the race. My shirt that morning read:

Power

Energy

Training

Endurance

Ready 2 Run!

At about Mile 15, a female runner came up alongside me and said, "I've been reading your shirt for the last eight miles! It's the only thing that's been keeping me going!" "I'm glad it helped you!" I replied. She responded, "Thanks for the motivation!" She then took off into the crowd of runners ahead of me! How's that for motivation? By using the power of words to inspire myself, I had also helped keep someone else going, giving her an extra boost in mental strength and endurance, just enough to … edge right past me!

I continued on, unruffled by the incident. I remember at one point, around Mile 20, saying my shirt's words to myself. I visualized myself as a powerful, energetic runner: "**Power**, **Energy**, **Training** …." Suddenly, I couldn't recall the next word. This really bothered me. Come on! What **was** that word? I couldn't see it since it was on my back. So I looked over and asked another runner, "What does my shirt say?" "Huh?" "What comes after 'Training'? I need to know!" He laughed and said, "**Endurance**! I could use some of that right now!" We both laughed.

On I went, mile after mile, until I looked up and saw a big red sign that read "Mile 25." This sign represented to me, at that moment, the promised land where milk and honey would flow. I felt a sudden burst of adrenaline rush through me. I was so close! I began to weave my way through people, feeling as though the race had finally begun for me. I then decided to take the advice of my crew coach in college, who always told us to "empty the tank." I let it all out with a mad dash to the finish line. I finally knew what it was like to feel glory and personal victory!

By visualizing every detail of the marathon, I was able to maintain my focus once I was actually running it. When you visualize the "look and feel" of your goals, you'll be motivated to see them through to completion.

POSITIVE VS. NEGATIVE VISUALIZATION

As you practice positive visualization, you'll begin to understand its tremendous power and influence on your life. But there's another side to the visualization coin — something we're all guilty of at one time or another: **negative** visualization, which is a direct result of negative self-talk.

Sometimes, you may find yourself unable to make progress on your goals. It is then that you need to ask yourself, "What might be holding me back from moving toward my vision?" Here are five of the most common vision blockers around:

- Fear,
- Self-doubt,
- A negative "inner critic,"
- Low self-esteem, and
- Conflicting voices.

Fear keeps you where you are. **Self-doubt** makes you question yourself and your abilities. Your **negative "inner critic"** is more than willing to tell you what you're incapable of doing. It haunts you anytime you try to stretch your comfort zone. **Low self-esteem** is rampant in our society and around the world, and it makes failure become a self-fulfilling prophecy. And **conflicting voices** speak to us when we try something new. Usually, the critic takes over and … well, you already know what the negative "inner critic" does!

Before you can make significant progress toward your vision, you must remove the barriers that stand in your way. One by one, you must knock down and eliminate the mental and emotional hurdles that block or blur your vision of the future.

When I was training for my first marathon, I heard all sorts of conflicting voices in my head. Let's call them the negative "Inner Critic" and the "Voice of Hope." A typical conversation went something like this:

Voice of Hope: "I know I can run 26.2 miles if I pour my heart and soul into it!"

Inner Critic: "You're crazy, man! What makes you think you can run a marathon? You've never run more than a mile in your whole life! And you're not much of an athlete, either."

Voice of Hope: "That may be true, but I know I can do anything I set my mind to."

Inner Critic: "You've really **lost** your mind. I'm about to have you committed."

Voice of Hope: "I already am committed — committed to my dream."

Fortunately for me, I decided to listen to the voice that convinced me (and my "Inner Critic") that it was possible to achieve my goal. I realized that my circumstances didn't have to define who I was or who I could become. My "Voice of Hope" continually told me that the only limitations I **really** had were the ones I might choose to place upon myself.

You've probably heard your own conflicting voices. If you haven't, you eventually will. When it happens, listen to the "Voice of Hope" that inspires you from within. Overpower your "Inner Critic" by continually feeding positive thoughts into your mind — through daily written and verbal affirmations.

A PATH OF POSSIBILITIES

When you outline a vision for yourself, you create possibilities for your life — possibilities that would not have existed unless you had first formed a mental picture of them. So when you write down your goals and make a list of your strengths and "growth areas," you pursue a path of possibilities. And when you sit back and daydream about what the future could hold for you, you pursue a path of possibilities. You become empowered by your vision — a vision no one can take away from you!

Create Your Vision

Developing a personal vision requires a certain amount of boldness. The act of envisioning involves looking beyond your current circumstances and opening yourself up to the great possibilities life has to offer. Envisioning a new future allows you to start breaking down the mental barriers you may have been building up for years, and to finally take ownership of your future.

What does your vision look like? What does it feel like? How real does it seem to you? Sit down and place your imaginary crystal ball in front of you:

One hundred years from now, how will people remember you? Will history record anything significant about your life?

You're on your deathbed. You've lived a long life. What are you most proud of? When did you really go out on a limb and take a risk? What is your greatest regret? If you could take just one more action to improve the world, what would it be? If you could tell someone one more thing, what would it be?

You're midway through your career. You're rolling along on autopilot. What changes would you like to make in your life?

You're just starting out in your career or transitioning into a brand new one. What decisions will you make?

When you're thinking about what your vision will be, start from the outcome and work your way backward. This approach creates a mental and emotional link between you and your vision by breaking the process down into a series of smaller goals.

Revise Your Vision

Sometimes, you need to modify your vision. Perhaps unforeseen circumstances have caused you to rethink your goal(s). Maybe you've become physically unable to follow through with your original plan. Maybe you've lost the desire, or you never really had it to begin with. Maybe you were simply following someone **else's** star! Regardless of the reason(s), you may find yourself heading in an entirely different direction than you'd previously imagined.

One day, when I was nine, I was walking down the street with my mom. We saw a Boy Scout pass by, so my mom asked me if I wanted to become a Boy Scout when I was older. I told her, "There is no way on earth I will ever become a Boy Scout." At that time, I didn't know much about the organization; I thought it consisted of a bunch of bullies who spent all of their time in the woods roughing it up. I didn't have a full picture of what Scouting was all about.

Seven years later, I became an Eagle Scout — the highest rank in Scouting!

Being involved in Scouting gave me the opportunity to travel to South Korea for the "World Jamboree," a gathering of some 20,000 Scouts from

120 countries around the world. I was fortunate to form many lasting friendships at that event and the many others, big and small, I attended during my years as a Scout. Opportunities for adventure and leadership came my way because of my active involvement in the organization.

At one point, I found myself standing on top of an 11,000-foot mountain overlooking the landscape of Colorado and New Mexico. I was part of a 12-member troop representing the New England area that had explored Philmont Scout Ranch in Cimarron, New Mexico. Our adventure took us on a 10-day, 100-mile backpacking expedition through the wooded trails, muddy slopes, and majestic peaks of New Mexico. Hiking up Baldy Mountain was a great accomplishment for each of us. Reaching the summit was a beautiful and humbling experience. As we walked around the summit's edge, we noticed a rusty metal container. It was a "time capsule." As we opened the cover, we found handwritten notes on small pieces of paper from people who had reached the mountaintop 20 and 30 years earlier. Those hikers had promised to one day ascend the mountain again with their sons!

Our perceptions — or misperceptions — can cloud our visions because we only see things as we **think** they are, not as they really are. None of the crowning moments I experienced in Scouting would have taken place if I'd stuck to my old, somewhat ignorant idea of what Scouting represented. Opening your eyes to all the possibilities will increase your ability to get the most out of life. If I had stayed with my original notion that Scouting would never be a part of my life, I would have missed out on friendships and experiences that have positively shaped who I am today. So make sure you're flexible about your life's vision. Be prepared to revise your plans from time to time.

"The marvelous richness of human experience would lose something of its rewarding joy if there were no limitations to overcome."
— HELEN KELLER

From Paris to the Poconos

Your vision can change dramatically — if you allow it to unfold, and to let it guide you as it changes colors, shapes, and directions. Trust your vision to lead you in the right direction. You won't regret it.

My wife and I spent several months planning our honeymoon. After considering many possible romantic venues, we settled on the idea of a two-week trip to Paris. We envisioned ourselves strolling past the Eiffel Tower and Arc de Triomphe, soaking up the sights and sounds of the romance capital of the world.

But just a couple of months before our wedding, we faced a dilemma: Hotel rooms in Paris were scarce, and our funds were limited. So we eventually came to the difficult conclusion that Paris didn't fit into our plans after all.

Giving up on Paris was heartwrenching, but it also opened us up to new possibilities. We ended up spending our honeymoon in the Love Capital of Pennsylvania — the Poconos. A far cry from Paris, but romantic just the same.

When you become too rigid about your vision, you may miss out on unforeseen opportunities — opportunities that could turn out to be even more memorable and satisfying than the ones you originally had.

Cherish Your Vision

As you take positive, concrete steps toward your vision, you need to start realizing that it's yours to cherish. We usually give priority in our lives to those things we hold dear to our hearts. So take pride in the gradual progress you make toward your vision. See it as your own personal masterpiece in progress!

I once gave a Toastmasters speech entitled, "Hold Onto Your Dreams." It featured a story about a young person who almost lost sight of his dreams. He was born and raised in a loving and supportive family. He grew up in a nurturing environment where he learned that anything was possible — the sky was the limit. As a young boy, he had great hopes and aspirations. He wanted to become President of the United States or ambassador to a foreign country. In his mind, there was no limit to what he could do or accomplish.

He went on to high school to study the classics. It was there that he fell in love with communication, discourse, and the exchange of ideas. He went on to study at a prestigious university. He seemed to be right on track to achieving his goals and dreams … until something happened: He entangled himself in a relationship with a person who was negative and controlling. When he'd share his goals and dreams with her, she would say, "What makes you think you can do that? You don't have any money. You don't have any connections. You're just a big dreamer. There's no substance to your goals!" With friends like that, who needs enemies?

The relationship continued in a downward spiral of anger and frustration until he reached rock bottom — the lowest point in his life. Then, one day, he experienced a reversal of fortune when he walked into a bookstore and came across a book entitled, *Live Your Dreams*. Those three small words resonated with him instantly. Working the midnight shift as a toll collector, he spent many cold, wintry nights reading the book's words of hope and inspiration.

Within six months of reading the book, he mustered up the courage to end the relationship that was neither healthy nor loving.

The person I was speaking about, I eventually told the audience, was me. The people in the crowd were then no longer listening to a story about some faraway, unknown person; instead, they were hearing a very personal account shared by the author of the experiences.

The primary message of my speech: Embrace your dreams ... cherish your dreams ... hold on to your dreams!

Safeguard Your Vision

At some point along your journey to success, you might find your dream under attack. You may encounter people who act as if their sole purpose in life is to tear down your dreams. They'll try to negate your efforts, and they'll often sap you of your time and energy. They may be your own friends or even your family members — people you thought you'd have cheering for you every step of the way. It can be quite a shock to find out that the people who supposedly have your best interests at heart really don't support your dreams; they ridicule your ideas and mock you instead.

Generally, other people will act this way because they feel jealous, insecure, or resentful around you. So if you truly care about your dream, then you must stand up and defend it when others attack it. Consider how you'd react if someone attacked your children or others you care about. Wouldn't you protect your loved ones from harm? Protect your dream at all costs from the coldness and bitterness of jealous, hateful people. Resolve to make your dream happen, no matter what! You need to realize that your dreams are more important than the opinions of those around you who have limited visions — those who can't see beyond the reality of their present circumstances, and who are incapable of crafting a vision of the future. **Don't put limits on your dreams!**

When you decide to safeguard your dreams and start working to make your vision a reality, you resolve to let nothing and no one prevent you from exercising your full potential.

Realize Your Vision

The final phase of pursuing your vision could take days, weeks, months, or even years, depending on what your goal is and what your timeframe is for achieving it. Sometimes, people don't see the results of their visions in their own lifetimes. But that shouldn't stop you (or them) from taking the first steps toward your dream.

In his inaugural address to the American people in January 1961, President John F. Kennedy boldly asserted his vision of world peace and an end to communism. He declared to America:

> "All this will not be finished in the first 100 days. Nor will it be finished in the first 1,000 days, nor in the life of this administration, nor even perhaps in our lifetime on this planet. But let us begin."

Dr. Martin Luther King, Jr., envisioned a country where people of all racial and ethnic backgrounds would coexist peacefully. In August 1963, he gave his famous and heart-gripping "I Have a Dream" speech to thousands of listeners on the steps of the Lincoln Memorial in Washington, D.C. His words were relentless; his passion indomitable. He imagined a day when human beings would judge each other "not by the color of their skin, but by the content of their character." Has King's vision materialized? One could argue that our society has made enormous progress toward improved racial relations in the United States and throughout the world. Yet we have so much more progress to make. King only **began** pursuing his vision, setting the pace for others to follow in the years and decades to come.

BECOME YOUR OWN "FORTUNETELLER"

Do you know any people who constantly rely on others to be their "fortunetellers"? They spill their life stories to people they hardly know, then allow (or even demand) those people to create their futures for them. Instead of taking responsibility for their own lives and their own current circumstances, they take the easy way out and let their fate be determined by someone else.

When you give others the power to run your life and dictate your future, you put yourself in a terrible spot. Your self-esteem goes out the window, as does your ability to make your own decisions and enhance the quality of your own life. You become unable to establish your own priorities in life because someone else is doing it for you.

Your vision is your blueprint for success. Many a blueprint has been tossed in the trash or hung out to dry. So what will make yours work? The answer: A compelling vision that you've developed for **yourself** — a vision so powerful, so colorful, so bold, so wonderful that you can't wait to get started on it. The more "personal" your vision, the more you'll be drawn to it and motivated to achieve it.

I was once called upon to be a "memory expert" while I was team leading a popular communications course. The technique I had learned that made me an expert on memory was to associate vivid mental pictures with what I was trying to remember. Most people think that having to recall more details will make it more difficult to remember something. But in reality, the opposite is true: Your mind has a greater capacity to remember things that are full of details, colors, adjectives, and exaggerations. So the more vivid your dream and the more colorful your vision, the greater the chance you'll succeed in achieving it.

MAKE YOUR VISION CRYSTAL CLEAR

History will always remember Eleanor Roosevelt for her famous phrase, "The future belongs to those who believe in the beauty of their dreams." When you believe in the magic and beauty of **your** dreams, the future will be yours for the taking. Life will indeed make room for you, allowing you to show your greatness to the world and leave it a better place than you found it.

The clearer your vision is to you yourself, and the more clearly you can convey it to the people around you, the greater your chances of actually transforming that vision into reality. Life always makes room for people who imprint their visions clearly in their minds and follow up with action.

Your Vision: Clear or Muddled?

The following examples illustrate a **clear vision** versus a **muddled vision**. See if you can decide which is which:

Example A

In five years, **I see myself** developing my very own consulting business in advertising. After completing my MBA in three years, **I will develop** a business plan to get my business up and running. **I will seek** the advice of top professionals in this field to make my vision a reality. Based upon the knowledge and expertise I've developed over the last eight years in the advertising world, **I will create** joint ventures with other consulting and marketing companies. **I will appear** on radio and television shows to discuss how my consulting company will be unique from any other of its kind. After just five years in this business, **I expect** to make my first million.

Example B

I hope to start my own consulting business at some point down the road. I'd like to be rich someday!

Do you see any differences between the first and second examples? The first person has clearly laid out a vision for accomplishing certain goals — a vision that includes specific details and timeframes. He's also used phrases like "I see myself," "I will develop," "I will seek," "I will create," "I will appear," and "I expect." All of these phrases express confidence and possibility. You must expect to achieve your goals, not wonder if they **might** happen when the planets and stars align just right!

"Where there is no vision, people perish."
— PROVERBS 29:18

The second person may have good intentions. Many people do. But the road to frustration is paved with them! Who do you think will be more likely to get a business up and running? Will it be the person who knows exactly what steps she wants to take toward her goal and when, or the person who has only a vague notion of what she wants to do and when?

Whenever we visualize a goal, we internalize potential outcomes in our mind. Our thoughts produce a mental picture of what we'd like to happen. If we continue focusing on our vision, it becomes a permanent fixture in our mind's eye until we finally take action to bring about the results we desire. Along the way, though, we must make decisions that will influence — for better or worse — what the outcome will be. So if you don't like the outcome, throw it out and try something else. Then re-evaluate your goals. It's never too late to change direction.

"Your values anchor your vision."
— PETER COLWELL

ALIGN YOUR VISION AND VALUES

The most important tool you have in life is your set of values. Our values are the qualities or ideals that help shape the outcomes of our lives. Some common values that people share are love, friendship, honesty, commitment, freedom, privacy, loyalty, citizenship, altruism, and self-expression.

Our families, leaders, and organizations instill values in us from an early age. Obedience, for instance, is one value most children are expected to live up to: "Obey your mother and father." "Listen to your teacher." "Do as I say, not as I do." "Wash your hands." "Brush your teeth." "Do your homework."

Another value we're all familiar with is justice. Justice is not only a personal value, but a national one as well. Our country places justice and fairness at the very top of its list of values. It's easy to find injustice around you, and there are many things you can do to help uproot it in your community and country. In fact, that's where the value of freedom of speech can be enormously helpful.

What do you value most in your relationships with others? in your business or professional life? in your personal or spiritual life? Think about your "Top 10 Values." Then write them down below, along with why each is so important to you:

WHAT I VALUE MOST	*WHY IT'S IMPORTANT TO ME*
______________________	______________________
______________________	______________________
______________________	______________________
______________________	______________________
______________________	______________________
______________________	______________________
______________________	______________________
______________________	______________________
______________________	______________________
______________________	______________________

There are three rules to remember when it comes to your values and your vision:

- Know your values.
- Fit your vision to your values.
- Never reverse this order.

Your values anchor your vision. Your values keep you grounded when you drift and stray. If you follow a vision of the future without concern for your values, you may very well end up unfulfilled and disillusioned. You might end up saying to yourself (as far too many people do): "I have the job I've always wanted. I'm finally comfortable financially. So why do I feel empty inside?"

Make sure your values and your vision are compatible. Determine their compatibility *before* your pursue your vision. In so doing, you'll ensure that your vision is right for you and that it will fulfill you.

We've come to your moment of truth. In three sentences, describe your vision in vivid detail. It should include where you live, what you do for a living, what you do in your spare time, and what your relationships are like:

____

____

____

____

____

____

____

Now, ask yourself: "Is this vision compatible with the personal values I included on my "Top 10 Values" list? Will following this vision create harmony in my life? Or will it cause conflict? Will I feel fulfilled? Or will I feel trivial?"

What Am I Doing Here?

Have you ever found yourself wondering out loud, "What am I **doing** here? How did I end up in a spot like this one? Someone must be playing a really mean trick on me. What did I ever do to deserve being treated this way by my boss/friend/lover?"

You can probably remember two or three times in your life when you saw the writing on the wall — writing that you ignored or refused to acknowledge for a long time. Then, one day, it hit you: You weren't living the life you had always wanted. You weren't making the best use of your time and talents. Instead, you were wasting precious time and energy doing something that didn't fulfill you!

It's at times like these when we (eventually) realize that our values and our vision are out of whack. We begin to see that it's time for a "tune-up" that includes a serious "realignment job." If your values and your vision are a good match, you're in good shape. But if they conflict with each other, you'll have to rethink your vision so that it better coincides with your beliefs and values. Only then will you be able to transform your vision into glorious reality!

POINTS TO REMEMBER

- Create your vision.
- Revise your vision.
- Cherish your vision.
- Safeguard your vision.
- Realize your vision.

SIX

SAVOR

Enjoy the Journey and the Destination

"Every person needs to have their moment in the sun, when they raise their arms in victory, knowing that in this day, at this hour, they were at their very best."

— H. JACKSON BROWN, JR.

A series of events comes together into one magical moment — the moment you've long been waiting for, when others take notice of your efforts and when the spotlight is suddenly on you. Your preparation and hard work, your endless visualizations of a positive outcome, and your boldness and passion have brought into the light your glorious achievement...

You've realized your dream! You've achieved your goal!

You have every right to take delight in this moment and cherish it. Maybe you've just crossed the finish line of a race. Maybe you've just walked across the stage to receive the degree you've been working for day and night. Maybe you've just bought your first home, or you've given birth to a child. Maybe you've just won a battle with cancer. Whatever your accomplishment, **Savor** it! You deserve to revel in your special accomplishment, and to soak in the praise and admiration of others (some of whom may have helped you along the way).

The moment of achievement represents the convergence of your **expectations** and the **reality** of your circumstances. Many times, your achievement will far outweigh your initial expectations. We generally call this phenomenon "succeeding beyond your wildest dreams." Sometimes, however, you'll fall short of your expectations and/or become disillusioned with the success you **are** experiencing. You might say to yourself, "Is this all it's cracked up to be? I thought my life would be so much different!"

Each aspiration you achieve in life will become a crowning moment when your goals, dreams, hopes, and expectations have come together, giving you a feeling of wholeness and unity and making your life worthwhile and fulfilling. Sometimes, though, you may not feel as thrilled with your success as you thought you would. That's why it's also important to learn how to stay grounded and patient with yourself. So let's talk about how (and how not!) to savor your success, and why it's important for you to do.

THANK YOUR "SUPPORTING CAST"

The success you experience is well deserved and the result of your dedication, vision, creativity, initiative, and desire. However, rarely does anyone achieve great things without the help, support, and encouragement of other people — the "supporting cast."

Every leading actor must be surrounded by a quality "supporting cast" to be successful. Every great athlete must play with dedicated, team-oriented colleagues in order to win championships. Take, for example, Larry Bird, the former perennial Most Valuable Player and All-Star for the Boston Celtics. During his 11 seasons with the Celtics, Bird was a part of three championship teams. While it's true that he often single-handedly elevated the morale of his teammates, he was fortunate to be surrounded by a cast of talented players. His unselfish style of play proved to be contagious, spreading through the whole team and the rest of the organization. The qualities of **unselfishness** and **teamwork** became the hallmark of the Boston Celtics tradition. That's why, with every achievement during his career, Bird always gave credit to his coaches and teammates, all of whom helped him become so successful.

Think about the people in your life who have made a difference in helping you achieve your goals — and indeed have helped shape who you are today: parents, friends, teachers, motivational speakers, colleagues, students, neighbors, family members, sports heroes, or virtual strangers.

Now, make a list of 10 people who have been influential in shaping your values, who have encouraged you when your heart was heavy, or who stood by you when times were tough:

____________________ ____________________

____________________ ____________________

____________________ ____________________

____________________ ____________________

____________________ ____________________

When you achieve the success you so richly deserve, be sure to show sincere gratitude to those who have helped you bring your goals to fruition. They, too, want to savor your accomplishments. Equally important, they deserve to celebrate their **own** roles in making your achievements a reality.

SAVOR THE UNEXPECTED MOMENTS

In the 2002 Winter Olympic Games in Salt Lake City, Sarah Hughes emerged as the surprising gold medal winner in the very popular — and very competitive — figure skating competition. Hughes, a 16-year-old high school junior from Great Neck, New York (a suburb of Long Island), found herself thrust into the spotlight when a series of missteps by her competitors not only placed her in contention for an Olympic medal, but launched her into first place when the judges tallied their scores.

Figuring she had no chance to win a medal, Hughes skated her heart out, dazzling the crowd and a worldwide television audience with seven triple jumps in her routine. After her performance, the audience gave her a long standing ovation.

Overwhelmed by the audience's positive reaction to her virtually flawless routine, Hughes started to exit the rink to await her scores. But her coach gently nudged her back onto the ice and yelled, "Soak it in, Sarah!" Hughes was able to savor the applause of the fans — and, shortly afterward, she got the chance to savor an unexpected victory as well!

Heavyweight Expectations

Here's one memory I have from my own life…

It was my freshman year at Georgetown University in Washington, D.C. As a kid, I had always dreamed about what it would be like to go to an

Ivy League school. As it turned out, though, I ended up at Georgetown, a school that's on par with many Ivy League institutions.

As a first-year student, I joined the Novice Heavyweight Crew Team. I had always thought it might be fun to row on the river, to become part of a team, and to experience the tranquility of an early-morning row. Well, I experienced many early-morning rows — some tranquil, some not so tranquil! During the fall season, I worked hard to get into top shape, hoping to qualify for the second boat — which would compete at the "Belly of the Carnegie" race in Princeton, New Jersey. I trained on the ergometers (simulated rowing machines), lifted weights regularly, ran stairs and hills, and watched my diet. In short, I did everything I could to prepare myself to row well in the race.

One morning, a week before the race, the team gathered around the boathouse while the coach announced the roster. He yelled out the last names of the guys who would be racing. The name "Colwell" was never called.

After a few days of dejection, I decided to look on the bright side: At least I had gotten into the best shape of my life up to that point. I was also improving as a rower, considering that I was brand new to the sport. So eventually, I decided to accompany the team to Princeton to cheer them on against the Ivy Leaguers, who were tough competitors. We took the bus up on a cool, crisp autumn morning in November, and set up the boats and oars. I stretched out with the team and wished them good luck.

Meanwhile, my own luck was about to change. About 20 minutes before the start of the race, my coach threw a long-sleeved shirt at me and yelled, "Pete, you're rowing for Columbia!" What? Was I hearing correctly? At the last minute, one of the lightweight rowers for Columbia University had gotten really sick, and he had to bow out. So there I was, throwing on a dark blue Columbia jersey and heading into a boat with seven rowers and a coxswain whom I'd never met. The key to rowing successfully is getting to know your teammates, learning to row in sync with them and developing a unified rhythm. This process usually takes place over the course of several weeks and months. I had to try and do it in several minutes! In addition, I was a heavyweight rower trying to row with lightweight rowers, whose strokes were shorter and quicker than mine.

As we warmed up along the river, all I could think was, "I have to have the row of my life, or these people are going to think I'm throwing the contest." Talk about pressure! We soon reached the starting point. I held on tight to my oar … and started pulling like a madman. We quickly gained on all the boats, first by half a boat length, then a full boat length. I kept telling myself, "Don't get your oar stuck." I concentrated on every stroke. As we passed under the bridge nearing the final 100 meters of the race, the coxswain yelled out to me, "Come on, 3 seat, **pull**!" We cleared the bridge and finished strong — ahead of my Georgetown teammates. When the boats came to a stop, I looked over at them and smiled!

What a day it turned out to be. I had come to root my team on, but instead I'd gotten to row for an Ivy League squad that ended up defeating my own squad. In the next couple of weeks that followed, I replayed that whole day in my mind — especially the race itself — visualizing how it felt to row in sync with the rest of my "new team." I also worked harder than ever to increase my strength and endurance. My efforts paid off: Within a couple of months, I had advanced to the second boat!

TAKE YOUR SUCCESS IN STRIDE

My Uncle Alfred once gave me some sage advice that I continue to use to this day: "Remember to always keep things on an even keel." At the time, he was referring to a crush I had on a girl I'd met at summer camp. While his words to me then were helpful as I tried to deal with my 12-year-old emotions, they've also proven to be beneficial since, in many areas of my life. I learned from an early age to take things in stride — to develop an air of nonchalance about the events in my life. It's not that I don't enjoy my personal and professional victories: I do! But I've learned, over time, to keep my successes and accomplishments "on an even keel" — to celebrate without getting a swelled head, and without forgetting my roots, my values, and my true sources of inspiration: My family, my friends, and my Creator.

What this also means is that I've learned to keep my failures and setbacks "on an even keel" as well. I don't allow temporary defeats or failed attempts to keep me down for long. Instead, I strive for moderation in my actions and thoughts so that I keep on that ever-so-important "even keel."

When I was applying to college, my first-choice school was Harvard University, a much-renowned institution. I felt I deserved admission into Harvard because of my scholarship in my studies, my dedication to community service, and my various other talents. So once I sent my application to the school, I eagerly awaited its reply. One Saturday morning a few weeks later, I found an envelope leaning out of our mailbox. I rushed downstairs and opened it with excitement. But inside was one solitary page that began with the phrase, "I regret to inform you … ." That was all I needed to read. I was crushed. I felt like I'd been whomped by a ton of bricks.

For the next few days, I was disappointed and dejected. But then I began to realize that I still had many other options to choose from. About a week later, I got another letter — this time from Georgetown University.

I slowly opened the envelope and read the first word: "Congratulations!" Once again, that was all I needed to read. I jumped up and down and shared the letter with my mom. Georgetown had accepted me not just for my academic performance, but because its decision makers felt I was well-rounded and showed potential in many areas.

I didn't let my victory go to my head, though! I just savored the feeling of being accepted to such a prestigious university.

This up-and-down (make that down-and-up) experience engraved in my mind an important lesson: In defeat, you must keep your head above water; in victory, you must keep your feet on the ground.

SAVORING IS A SKILL YOU CAN LEARN

Achieving your goal doesn't complete the process of succeeding. After all, your life isn't over once you become a millionaire, and your challenges don't vanish once you've got your own house and a dream job.

We often get caught in the trap of rushing from one moment to the next without taking the time to absorb the impact of our achievements and appreciate their value. Many people, in fact, minimize the significance of their accomplishments and instead watch as their lives become a big blur. Are you one of them?

After I won a speech contest one night — at which I discussed many of the topics covered in this book — a distinguished gentleman with a British accent came up to me in the parking lot and congratulated me for my performance. I thanked him, but the only thing on my mind was how I was going to prepare for the next competition the following week. He must have noticed the distracted look on my face, because he said, "Be sure to **savor** it!" I took his words to heart and made a concentrated effort to enjoy the moment. I treated myself to an ice cream sundae and replayed the speech in my mind, picturing the smiles on the faces in the audience. It felt great reliving my performance. If I hadn't run into that man, I probably would have rushed home and gone to bed or, worse, started practicing too early for my next competition.

The following passage has inspired me through tough times and joyful times because of its message of accepting what life gives us and making the most of it:

The Secret of Living

Make each day a magnificent adventure,
Accept the challenges that come your way,
Seize each opportunity that you find,
Without concern for what others might say.
Experience each day with open arms,
Savoring both victory and strife,
Welcoming the good and bad together,
For only then will you know the joy of life.
— Anonymous

FIVE WAYS TO SAVOR YOUR SUCCESS

You know you deserve to pause and savor your success. But how do you go about doing it? Here are some effective ways to soak in those finer moments in your life when you are at your very best — moments that make your efforts worthwhile:

Celebrate Your "Mini-Milestones" along the Way

Depending on the nature and complexity of your goals, it may take you a while for you to reach the proverbial "finish line." So to stay motivated and inspired along the way, celebrate your "mini-milestones" as you achieve them.

If your long-term goal, for example, is to write a romance novel, celebrate the completion of each chapter by treating yourself (and perhaps your supportive spouse or significant other) to a fancy meal, or simply relaxing from your ordinary daily routine. Or maybe you want to become president of a university someday. If so, celebrate smaller milestones, like earning a graduate degree or landing an administrative job within the university, or even less ambitious milestones, like completing an intensive seminar on executive leadership.

By celebrating your "mini-milestones," you'll be more apt to stay on track toward your long-range goals — without burning out before you achieve them.

Try "Post-Visualization"

If you're a natural goal setter and go-getter, then you know you have to visualize your way to your goals. You probably also realize the importance of basking in your success, at least for a while. You've got the "pre-game" and the "game" covered, but what about the "post-game show?" Don't forget to relive your achievements from time to time.

Maybe your accomplishment was videotaped. If so, watch a few "reruns" of your successful event. I love to sit back and relish my past victories. Recently, for example, I gave a prize-winning presentation in a very competitive speech contest. The pressure was enormous, but my adrenaline was working in my favor. I was "on" from the moment I stepped onto the stage. The audience felt it and so did I. So every now and then, I pop in a videotape of that speech and relive that great moment.

As a child, you may have been "preconditioned" by your parents and teachers not to "toot your own horn." You may have been taught that "self-promotion" is selfish, and that people shouldn't talk about themselves too much. But savoring your success doesn't mean you need to flaunt your talents and boast about your big wins. Instead, you can enjoy your accomplishments by soaking in the good feelings and remembering them the next time you're pursuing a worthy goal.

Keep a "Success Journal"

One way to treasure your accomplishments is to keep a record of them in a "success journal." You may come up with a fancier name for it, like "dream diary" or "performance portfolio." The idea is still the same: Just start collecting mementos of your success — clippings from articles written by or about you, prizes and awards you've earned, and the like. Include a log of your personal thoughts before, during, and after each of the successes you document so that you can "replay" those moments later and feel good (again!) about what you've done.

Reward Yourself Each Week

You'll only stay on target toward achieving your goals if you reward yourself regularly. So make it a habit to give yourself a little "prize" of some sort at the end of each week, especially if you've had an unusually tough week. Knowing that a reward is in sight (even if that reward is self-constructed) will prevent you from "slacking off" or "blowing off" your work altogether.

Share Your Successes with Others

What's the first thing you want to do when you accomplish something you're really proud of? If you're like most people, you want to tell the world about it. I know that whenever I have a success, the first thought that runs through my head is, "Where's the phone so I can call my wife … and my mom and dad … and my sister … and my friends?"

Sharing your successes is not a gloat-fest or a "look-at-me-I'm-great" tactic. It simply allows others to celebrate vicariously through your efforts — and it may even inspire other people in your life to pursue their own goals.

ENJOY THE JOURNEY AND THE DESTINATION

By now, you've realized that at least half of the fun involved in succeeding is striving to **get to** your destination; the other half comes from actually **getting there**. So when you do reach your goal — whether it be a richer or healthier existence, or a life without emotional clutter and needless anxiety — you owe it to yourself to savor your achievement. Take time to reflect on it and what it means to you. Before you start wrestling with the "what's next?" question, slow down and enjoy the fruits of your labor. Don't let your eagerness to rush toward the next goal or reach for the next level of success prevent you from basking in your **current**, here-and-now accomplishment!

POINTS TO REMEMBER

- Thank your "supporting cast."
- Take your success in stride.
- Savor the unexpected moments.
- Savoring is a skill you can learn.
- Savor your successes, both during the journey and once you reach your destination.

SEVEN

SOAR

Build on your success

"One can never consent to creep when one feels an impulse to soar."

— HELEN KELLER

The realization of a dream awakens within you the magic of your personal power: The power to set and achieve exciting and challenging goals … the power to evaluate your assets and liabilities … the power to create an extraordinary life for yourself regardless of the memories of your past or the circumstances of your present … the power to condition your mind to think positively, to increase your level of fitness, and to harness your emotions so that they work in your favor … the power to clearly envision what you want your life to be all about … the power to appreciate and savor the high points of your success and every step that got you there … and, most importantly, the power to **Soar** — to spread your wings and see where else they'll take you!

Success occurs in waves. You reach a high point when you're at your peak. Then you come crashing back to the sandy reality of daily activities. But no matter where you are or whatever particular wave you're riding at a given moment, you always need to be looking forward to the future — and thinking about ways to keep it satisfying and fun.

KEEP CHALLENGING YOURSELF

One sure way to keep your life exciting and rewarding is to continuously challenge yourself. For years, I have carefully observed people, sometimes to the point of feeling like I'm a closet sociologist. I marvel at people's behaviors and reactions to different situations. Through my "research," I've found that people who usually sit around and do nothing generally have blank or despondent looks on their faces. People who convey intensity and purpose, on the other hand, walk around with a sense that they are **somebody**! They've got some place to go or some important thing to accomplish. While it's impossible to read people's minds, their body language often communicates their thoughts, feelings, and attitudes loudly and clearly.

"A life without goals is not worth living."
— JUDY BLUME

At some point in your climb toward success, you'll reach a level of proficiency and perhaps even mastery of whatever it is you're doing. With proficiency and mastery can come familiarity and comfort: You're in your "comfort zone," where things are quite familiar to you. At first, that can be great. You're an expert, you're on top of your game, and life is good. But eventually, you reach a plateau. And you lose that one important element that brings excitement to your life — a challenge!

STRETCH YOUR SUCCESS

Being content to stay where you are may feel like the comfortable thing to do. But if you don't stretch yourself from time to time, you may never know the pleasure of finding out exactly what you're capable of. So here are six ways to "stretch your success":

Accept a Leadership Role

At some point in your life, you'll be presented with the prospect of serving in a leadership role (e.g., president of the PTO, Scoutmaster, club leader, chair of an advisory board). Pursue one or more of these endless opportunities. When you do, the spotlight will be on **you**. People will look to you to initiate discussions, create agendas, make decisions, and take responsibility. What better way for you to assert yourself, tap your creativity, and grow personally or professionally?

Take a Stand on Issues You Feel Strongly About

Deep down, we all feel strongly about something, whether it's preserving natural resources or wildlife, preventing crime, fighting air pollution, or keeping "Sesame Street" on public television. Maybe it's not a community issue that stirs you, but certainly there is **something** you have deep-seated convictions about. Whether it's an injustice in this unfair world or simply a pet peeve, stand up and speak out on it. You just might have a positive impact on the situation you're trying to change. At the very least, you'll gain courage and self-confidence by daring to voice your opinions.

Express Yourself in a New Way

Sometimes, you can fall into the trap of being one-sided — of not showing the many sides of your personality. We all have parts of us that are a little shy, parts that are wild and audacious, parts that are polite, and parts that are just downright crazy. Don't you just love it when you meet someone who brings out another side of you, especially a side that's been hidden for a while? Often, we fall in love with people because they bring out the "hidden" aspects of our personality. So stretch your success by expressing yourself in a different way. People will be quite surprised to see other sides of you.

In Toastmasters, I've given many speeches on rather serious topics, such as personal power and the importance of holding onto your dreams. At one point, I realized that a lot of people in the group thought of me as "Mr. Serious." I knew there was another side of me that they weren't aware of. So, one day, I gave a presentation dressed in a flowered Hawaiian shirt with a lei wrapped around my neck. I interpreted the classic Dr. Seuss book, *Oh, the Places You'll Go!* I pranced around the room, contorting my body and doing all kinds of funny voices, changing my pitch and tone throughout. People saw that day that I could also be funny and laugh at myself. It felt great to express myself in a different way!

Take Chances

Life is a risky game. There are no easy answers. We never have a 100 percent guarantee of success when we set out to do something. Many people avoid failure by simply avoiding risks. But you have to take chances if you want to reach your goals. I took a big chance, for instance, when I set out on my first marathon. I had only prepared for the event for five months, and I didn't have any previous marathon experience. I trained mostly by myself and therefore relied on self-motivation to complete my training. My family and friends had come from other states to watch me run, and they were filled with excitement and anticipation — both of which I had helped create: "You've got to come see me run in a marathon!" "I want you there at the finish line!" What if I didn't make it to the finish line? What if I ran out of steam before Mile 26? Those were daunting questions, but I was willing to take the chance on myself.

Break Your Usual Pattern

Have you ever noticed yourself slogging through the same routine day after day after day? While routine lends stability to your life, it can also stagnate you and keep you from advancing in your career. Too much of one thing dulls your mind and dampens your spirit. One simple way to alleviate this problem is to break your usual pattern. Take a longer lunch than normal. Sleep in some morning. Cancel an appointment. Try a new food. Take a mini-vacation at a moment's notice. Do **something** to break out of the "rut" you've gotten yourself into. When you break your usual pattern, you show yourself and others that you have the courage to step out of the comfort of your day-to-day routine.

Develop New Relationships

The people around you are key to your success because they can help you achieve your goals — or do just the opposite. Find the right people and your life can (and probably will) take off. Find the wrong people, however, and you're as good as done: You can forget about your dreams. Your energy will be sucked right out of you. You'll start to see all kinds of huge obstacles in your path, and you'll begin to tell yourself that living your dreams is just too hard. You will say to yourself, "It's just not possible!" And once you determine that something is impossible, your mind will automatically shut off all mental and emotional channels that could actually make it a reality.

So cultivate positive relationships with people who bring out star-like qualities in you, and who will help you progress toward your goals.

COMING BACK TO EARTH

You've reached your noble goal. Your dream has come true. Now what?

Perhaps the toughest part of achieving momentous and long-awaited success is the need to eventually return to your normal, everyday life. It's very natural (and common) to experience feelings of emptiness and perhaps even depression after weeks, months, or even years of anticipation and emotional build-up on the way to your moment of success.

Think of the astronaut who goes to the moon: After standing on a celestial, faraway landscape most of us can only dream of, the astronaut must then return to what, by comparison, must be a very mundane existence. What about the politician who spends countless hours, days, and months blazing the campaign trail ... or the person who trains day and night, year after year, in hopes of Olympic glory ... or the couple who pour their heart and soul into planning the ultimate wedding day? All of these types of situations involve enormous amounts of preparation, training, and conditioning — blood, sweat, and tears; highs and lows; pleasure and pain; ecstasy and disappointment. Yet, the outcome is never certain. Victory is never a guarantee.

But once your quest for a certain goal is over — whether you win or lose — you must learn to handle success **and** temporary failure equally well, by keeping that "even keel" we discussed in Chapter 6 and by preparing yourself mentally and emotionally for your next venture.

3 Strategies for Perpetuating Success – and Staying Grounded

Countless stories have been told about people who "let success go to their head." Through my own observations and experiences, I've come up with three strategies you can use to stay grounded during times of enormous, superhuman achievement:

Focus on Areas That Still Need Work

No matter how proficient you become at what you do, it's safe to say that you can still improve in certain areas. Larry Bird and Michael Jordan, for instance, are two icons of professional basketball. One thing these two players had in common was a relentless desire to better their best.

I remember reading in 1986, an article in a sports magazine about Larry Bird, with the headline, "The Best Gets Even Better." The story was about Bird's decision to go back home to French Lick, Indiana, the summer after winning the NBA World Championship to work on his game. Incredibly, one of the world's all-time greatest basketball players, who had mastered the psychological and physical aspects of the game, was going back to his roots to perfect and fine-tune his skills. What an incredible role model for perpetual success! Bird never let fame, fortune, or phenomenal success cloud his vision of personal greatness. Mentally speaking, he was always two or even three steps ahead of his opponents. On the heels of victory, he consistently looked forward to the next competition.

Another extraordinary example of someone who continually taps into his potential is Michael Jordan, undoubtedly one of the world's greatest all-around athletes. Jordan has always refused to settle for being a great slam dunker or jump shooter. He has worked tirelessly to become a great shot blocker, defender, and long-range shooter as well. He wants to be known not as a one-sided player, but as an all-around team player.

Encapsulate Your Achievements

It's far too easy to connect your very identity with your job, position, status, or achievements — and to set yourself up for disappointment in the process. What happens, for example, when you get fired, demoted, downsized, or overlooked for recognition or promotion? You feel your very **essence** has been rejected. You take it personally, don't you?

We all tend to identify ourselves by our past achievements — e.g., earning a Ph.D., being named "Salesman of the Year," completing a marathon. But when we rely upon our past accomplishments to automatically lead to future success, we run the risk of disillusionment and eventual failure. One way to avoid this potential problem is to look at your achievements as cherished moments of the past. Hold them dear to your heart, and reflect upon them to build your confidence for future projects — but leave them in the **past**. No matter how much you've excelled in a certain area, you must continue to challenge yourself and prove yourself. Don't make the common mistake of allowing yourself to become too comfortable. Instead of adopting a *laissez-faire* approach to your future endeavors, develop the mindset that your learning curve is continuous and never-ending.

Multi-purpose Your Mission

Successful people **diversify** — they "multi-purpose" their personal missions. Take Dick Clark, for instance. This famous television personality is known for his ability to entertain, but he does so in many different ways. He started out as host of "American Bandstand" in the 1950s, which became a national hit for many years. He was later host of the popular game show, "The $25,000 Pyramid." He didn't stop there. He has emceed Miss America pageants, promoted the Publishers Clearing House Sweepstakes with Ed McMahon, and, perhaps most memorably, helped us ring in many a New Year's Day with "Dick Clark's New Year's Rockin' Eve!" On top of all that, he runs his own successful production company.

Clark's perpetual success is attributable to his ability to multi-purpose his skills. Suppose he'd decided he could only be successful as the host of a television music show on Saturday mornings. He would have lost opportunities to do commercials, host specials and game shows, and run his own business. Eventually, he probably would have retired from the business he is so passionate about.

Have **you** come up against a roadblock? Then, move in another, similar direction. Use your skills to achieve your goals in a different way. You might find that your new path is equally or even more enjoyable. And you might be even more effective than you would have been because you'll be tapping into talents that have been "hidden" to you in the past.

"Don't suppress yourself by your perceived limitations! The only limitations you really have are the ones you choose to place upon yourself!"
— PETER COLWELL

So, you want to be an actor? How about being an actor, singer, model, and keynote speaker? Why stop at just being an actor? Develop and use your other talents too.

So, you want to write books? How about speaking on the topic(s) you write about, teaching classes in your area of expertise, and consulting with people who need your help? Why limit yourself to just writing books?

So, you want to be a professional athlete? What about pursuing another passion in the off-season — like contributing to charities, or starting clinics to teach and inspire kids who want to follow up in your footsteps?

So, you want to run for public office? What about teaching part-time as well … and mentoring others who aspire to public service … and promoting your cause in other tangible ways?

What happens when you multi-purpose your mission? You stay motivated, engaged, and productive. You develop yourself fully. And you never run out of ways to make a difference in your life and the lives of others.

CHART YOURSELF A NEW COURSE

I think of life as a choose-your-own-adventure story. Life is full of twists and turns, changes and challenges. Every decision we make acts as a compass that influences the direction our life is going to take next. In Chapter 1, I talked about taking responsibility for your life and becoming the "navigator in your own journey." If you don't like where your life is heading, it's not too late to change direction. In fact, it's never too late!

You'll find great joy in charting a new course for your life. Try things you've never tried before. You may discover talents you never knew you had, or achieve goals you dreamed about but never thought you'd bring to fruition in this lifetime. My sister Susan and I love to motivate each other. We're only two years apart, so we were very close growing up and are even more so today. We both have fiery, independent spirits and believe in the beauty of a dream. We see possibilities where other people see roadblocks. We enjoy saying to each other, "Just because you've never done something before **doesn't** mean you can't do it now," because it epitomizes how we feel about life. We love to do things precisely **because** we've never done them! We don't believe in limitations, because our parents taught us there's no such thing as limitations on our ability to dream.

If you can't count on support from your family, or if you don't have a family, you can still seek help — from counselors, close friends, or support groups, all of whom can help you develop a new path for your life. Find people who will encourage you to "stay on track" as you move in new directions.

Since writing this book, I have trained for and completed two marathons. Prior to these events, I had never run more than a couple of miles. I'd never even run in a 5K race! I'd never been a member of the track or cross-country teams in high school or college, either. But I didn't allow those facts to stand in my way. I was already halfway to my goal when I realized it was possible — that I could run 26.2 miles if I poured my heart, soul, and body into achieving the feat. My simple formula for achieving my goal was:

CONDITIONING + POSITIVE ATTITUDE + PERSISTENCE = SUCCESS

The majority of the tasks we set out to do in life are things we've never done before. I'd never written a book before. But as you can now plainly see, my inexperience didn't prevent me from writing one!

No matter how old or young you are, continue to stretch in new directions, explore new avenues, and expand your comfort zone. Only then will you come to realize the ever-growing possibilities for your life!

HOW TO COPE WITH SUCCESS

Some people have a difficult time dealing with the attention success brings to their lives. Others handle success very well and don't allow it to change their attitudes or behaviors. We hear comments about this latter group all the time: "Success hasn't changed her a bit." "She's still the same girl she always was." "Fame hasn't ruined her."

On the surface, you'd think that success wouldn't be something you'd have to **cope** with. It ought to be a pleasurable experience resulting from hard work and dedication to a specific goal, right? Then why do so many people get "ruined" by success? Do they simply let it "go to their head," or is something else happening?

My model for success is one in which you develop a high level of self-worth, you set worthwhile goals, you do whatever it takes to reach those goals, you take pleasure in your success when it comes, and you continue to explore the different parts of yourself and challenge yourself instead of "resting on your laurels." So when success comes your way:

- Avoid complacency. It can be your "worst enemy" when trying to create future successes.
- Always have your next goal in mind to keep you continuously motivated.
- Know that any outcome, good or bad, does not say anything about your self-worth.

When it comes to building on your successes, you need to be willing to endure a certain amount of discomfort along the way to your goals. You can't expect to train for and complete a triathlon, for example, without going through some aches and pains in the preparation process. To truly experience the joys of life, you must be willing to put up with the "pangs of success." You must be prepared for loss, sacrifice, growth, change, detours, the unexpected, setbacks, rejection, and disillusionment. If you can handle these and the many other "pangs" you'll likely face, then you're mentally and emotionally equipped for a lifetime of success. But that doesn't sound too rosy, does it?

The "road to success" is, in reality, an endless journey. One night, my wife (who knows intimately my philosophy of success) and I were discussing what success means to us individually and as a couple, in terms of both our current circumstances and our future expectations. We'd been married for only a few months at the time. At one point in the conversation, I squeezed Trevia lovingly and said, "As husband and wife, we must be prepared for stormy weather, heartache, setbacks, frustration, and disappointment. Are you up for the challenge, honey?" "You bet I am!" she replied. Wow! That wasn't exactly an ode to the utopic life. And it certainly wasn't your typical conversation between newlyweds!

Through my relentless study of the psychology and nuances of success, perhaps my greatest realization has been that success is really about developing and eventually having the confidence to make important, life-changing decisions and to take concrete action so that you can one day reflect upon your past with very few regrets.

Once you reach what you think of as "the height of success," you may be exactly where you figured you'd be someday. If you're like many people, however, you might get to "the height of success" only to discover that your life is out of balance, or that you've attained your goals but you haven't found fulfillment. What then? Here are some questions you may want to ask yourself to assess your situation:

- Is this what I wanted?
- Is this what I want now?
- What exactly do I want?
- What would I like to be different about my life?
- What can I do to change my circumstances?
- What's my next step?

"Every human being is a success story waiting to happen."
— PETER COLWELL

Now What?

A professional football player wins the Most Valuable Player award and the Super Bowl in the same year. A journalist approaches him and asks, "Now that you've won the MVP and the Super Bowl, what are you going to do?" If you've watched enough television, you know that the expected response is, "I'm going to Disney World!" But what is that player **really** going to do? Maybe the answer is, "Win another Super Bowl!" Many people don't know how to cope with the sudden emptiness they often feel after experiencing enormous success. Sometimes they even squander their fortune and prosperity and engage in self-destructive behaviors. Just watch a few episodes of VH1's "Behind the Music" program to see what I mean. This show describes the rise and fall of many child and young adult superstars who soaked in success "too much too soon," without preparing for it, and wound up in jail, on drugs, or in even worse situations.

How can you prevent these sorts of things from happening to **you** when **you** achieve success? The best method I know is to stay grounded and stay hungry. What happens when you feast on food over the holidays — one giant meal after another? You no longer crave that turkey or ham, do you? All of a sudden, the thought of another slice of pumpkin pie loses its appeal. Sometimes, too much of a good thing can spoil you. Too much success — all at once — can "go to your head." So when you achieve incredible goals, remind yourself of your roots. Remember what propelled you to stardom or what inspired you to rise from the ashes of poverty to the comfortable life you now live. Just as you did when you began your journey, take inventory of yourself once again. Reflect on your success and ask yourself some important questions:

- What events or circumstances in my life led me to where I am today?
- What was the driving force in my life that kept me going when times were tough?
- How can I draw on my past successes to lead myself to future successes?
- What have I learned along the way that can help me through the difficult times I might face in the future?
- How can I share my success with others?

Right now, you might be asking yourself (and me!), "How can I stay 'grounded' while maintaining the high level of motivation I need to pursue my dreams?" What I like to do is "make myself thirsty." I put myself in situations in which I can maintain my desire to achieve breakthroughs in my life by surrounding myself with people who want the same thing in their lives. In other words, when you play with the best, you become **your** best.

When I was a kid, I would shoot baskets in our back yard and at the city playground. I'd bounce the basketball from the moment I got home from school until it became dark. On weekends, I'd be the first one out there practicing my lay-ups and the last one out there working on my dribbling. One cold winter day when I was 12, I played in the rain. I was used to playing in the rain, so it didn't matter to me. Soon, though, the rain became freezing pelts of ice. But I played on, ignoring my mom's calls to come inside. Eventually, Mother Nature had the last word and I knew I had to head inside. So I turned around and made a left-handed hook shot. But the ball didn't go through the net because the net had suddenly become a string of icicles. I couldn't reach the hoop to punch the ball, so I had to borrow someone's umbrella and whack the net many times to get the ball out. I took what happened as a sign to head home and stop playing for a while!

As a child, I was relentless about the game of basketball. In the same way, you must be relentless about your goals and dreams if you want to make them come true. Through constant practice and a love of the game, I became an excellent basketball player. My success came not just from repetition and visualization, but also from playing with people who were older, taller, and usually more experienced than me. Sometimes, I'd even play against two or three other people to test myself even more. That way, when game time came, I was more than ready to handle someone my own age and height. I stayed hungry for basketball success by putting myself in challenging situations practically every day. You can stay hungry for your own form(s) of success by consistently challenging yourself the same way — by putting yourself in new and unexpected situations and doing the very things that scare you the most.

"Show me a thoroughly satisfied man
and I will show you a failure."
— THOMAS EDISON

SUCCESS: THE JOURNEY THAT NEVER ENDS

My ninth-grade English teacher, Lorraine Ashe, wrote a message to me when I earned the Eagle Scout award, the highest rank in Scouting: "It is the attempt to soar that represents the noblest nature in all of us." I used that quote in my high school yearbook, and those words have stuck with me to this day. It is not the soaring, but the **attempt** to soar, that really adds immeasurable value to your life. Nothing should stop you from **attempting** to do great things. You may not **achieve** everything you set out to do, but you'll be a better person for having tried.

By staying focused on your goals, you can build a positive self-image, attain peace of mind, conquer your fears, improve practically every area of your life, and still remain humble and true to yourself when all is said and done. By realizing that success is a lifelong journey from one stepping stone to another — a continuous learning and growing process — you can and will achieve self-fulfillment.

I hope you take something special away from this book, whether it's an idea, an empowering belief, or a new approach to an old situation. I hope you also realize that the road to success never has to reach a **dead end**. Use your God-given talents. Identify what you can contribute to others, then decide how you'll do that. Resolve to take action and you will do incredible things with your life. You can make your life all you want it to be and more. But it's all up to you!

Let me know how you're doing on your journey by visiting my website at www.petercolwell.com. As Lily Tomlin once said, "Success is a road that is always under construction." So start building the life of your dreams — and then keep on building as you spell "SUCCESS" in your life again … and again … and again.

Afterword

When you love self-improvement books (or any books, for that matter) as much as I do — both as a consumer and as a book editor — you want very badly to believe in what the authors of such books write, and in who they are as people. Unfortunately, it's usually easy to be disappointed on both counts. I have read and edited enough books to know that — as an exasperated book-editor friend said to me recently — "No, there is **not** a book inside of everyone!" Many books are, in fact, very poorly written. But far worse, they are penned by people who **say** they care about what they're doing and its impact on their readers, but who don't demonstrate it in their execution or in the way they live their own lives.

It is with all of this in mind that I have some wonderful news for you: Peter Colwell can write — and, more importantly, he truly **cares** about his life-changing work, and about helping you succeed in whatever endeavors you choose to pursue.

How do I know this? It's all in the evidence that has emerged over the course of the several months Peter and I have worked on this project together. I told Peter from the very beginning that if he was looking for a "yes man" editor — someone who would simply read through his book and "wave it on through" — I was definitely not his guy. But Peter didn't want a rubber stamper; he wanted to be challenged. And that is exactly what I've done throughout the extensive editing process that has culminated in the book you now hold in your hands.

At times when I was reading his stuff, I would say to Peter (and I meant this in the nicest possible way, of course!), "Peter, if I were a reader, my 'B.S. Meter' would be going into the 'code red' zone right now." Like all authors, myself included, Peter could at times become "too close" to what he was writing and lose the message he was trying to convey. When that happened, I pointed it out to him.

Peter could have simply ignored my comments (as many of the other authors I've worked with have), but instead he took them to heart and rewrote, revised, and revamped — often adding specific examples in the process to better illustrate the point(s) he was trying to make. It didn't take me long to realize that Peter knows **himself** well, and that he actually practices the keep-setting-goals-and-keep-achieving advice he so eloquently writes about in this book.

Peter and I walked our back-and-forth editing path through every word and sentence in this book. I raised with him every question that popped into my mind. Peter could have given up anywhere along the way and said, "Well, that's good enough." But he didn't — and that's why I can tell you with certainty that he cares about you and your success. He's passed **my** many tests with flying colors, and as you'll see when you read the "What Other People Are Saying..." section of the book (if you haven't already done so), I'm not alone when I think to myself, "Someday, we're going to say, 'We knew Peter when...'"

So enjoy the fruits of Peter's long labor, knowing that *Spell SUCCESS in Your Life* isn't "just another book" by just another "guru" who seems far removed from real life. Rest assured that there is a genuine, passionate, and thorough person behind the information you'll find in these pages — a person named Peter Colwell who will make a positive difference in your life and in the lives of many others.

Peter Vogt
Editor
Spell SUCCESS in Your Life

Helpful Resources

MOTIVATIONAL/SELF-HELP RESOURCES

Live Your Dreams, Les Brown (William Morrow & Co., 1993)
It's Not Over Until You Win!, Les Brown (Fireside, 1998)
www.lesbrown.com

How to Win Friends and Influence People, Dale Carnegie (Pocket Books, 1994)
How to Stop Worrying and Start Living, Dale Carnegie (Pocket Books, 1985)
www.dale-carnegie.com

The Road Less Traveled, M. Scott Peck (Simon & Schuster, 1998)
www.mscottpeck.com

Don't Sweat the Small Stuff ... and It's All Small Stuff, Richard Carlson (Hyperion, 1997)
www.dontsweat.com

Awaken the Giant Within, Anthony Robbins (Fireside, 1993)
www.tonyrobbins.com

The Millionaire's Secrets, Mark Fisher (Fireside, 1997)

The Power of Positive Thinking, Norman Vincent Peale (C.R. Gibson & Company, 1970)

Take Time for Your Life, Cheryl Richardson (Broadway Books, 1999)
www.cherylrichardson.com

The Life You Imagine, Derek Jeter (Crown Publishing, 2001)

Feel the Fear and Do It Anyway, Susan Jeffers (Fawcett Books, 1992)
www.susanjeffers.com

CAREER RESOURCES

Connecting with Success, Kathleen Barton (Davies-Black Publishing, 2001)

Do What You Are, Paul D. Tieger and Barbara Barron-Tieger (Little Brown, 2001)
www.personalitytype.com

Making a Living Without a Job, Barbara J. Winter (Bantam, 1993)

The Career Guide for Creative and Unconventional People, Carol Eikleberry (Ten Speed Press, 1999)
www.creativecareers.com

What Color is Your Parachute?, Richard N. Bolles (Ten Speed Press, 2002)
How to Find Your Mission in Life, Richard N. Bolles (Ten Speed Press, 2001)
www.jobhuntersbible.com

Whistle While You Work, Richard J. Leider and David A. Shapiro (Berrett-Koehler Publishers, 2001)
www.inventuregroup.com

PUBLISHING RESOURCES

The Self-Publishing Manual, Dan Poynter (Para Publishing, 2002)
www.parapublishing.com

How to Get Happily Published, Judith Appelbaum (HarperCollins, 1998)
www.happilypublished.com

The Complete Guide to Self-Publishing, Marilyn and Tom Ross (F&W Publications, 2001)
Jump Start Your Book Sales, Marilyn and Tom Ross (F&W Publications, 1999)
www.marilynandtomross.com

The Prepublishing Handbook, Patricia J. Bell (Cat's Paw Press, 1992)
www.catspawpress.com

Make Money Self-Publishing, Suzanne P. Thomas (Gemstone House Publishing, 2000)

About the Author

Peter Colwell is an award-winning motivational speaker, writer, and publisher with a magical message: That there is greatness within every one of us. As a member of Toastmasters International, he has excelled in the art of competitive speaking. His motivational writing has earned the praise and endorsements of many top international figures, including radio/TV personality and author Les Brown, business speaker and self-made millionaire Brian Tracy, and co-creator of the phenomenal *Chicken Soup for the Soul*® series Mark Victor Hansen.

Peter earned a Bachelor of Science degree in languages and linguistics from Georgetown University in 1997. Soon after graduation, he enrolled in the Dale Carnegie Course in Effective Speaking and Human Relations. After completing the program, he became a Graduate Assistant, coaching students of all ages in the art of effective speaking.

Peter's love of government has also led him to work at the Massachusetts State House, the Office of Senator Edward M. Kennedy (D-Mass.), the Department of Justice, and Ernst & Young Government Relations.

Peter has addressed all types of audiences, including corporate professionals, civic leaders, military personnel, nonprofit organizations, and high school students. Out of a pool of 10,000 contestants worldwide, Peter advanced to the semifinal round of the Toastmasters International Speech Contest in June 2000, prevailing as one of the top 72 speakers in the world. The speech that propelled him to those heights was based on the principles in *Spell SUCCESS in Your Life*.

As President of Motivational Magic, Peter offers keynotes, workshops, and seminars on the subjects of self-motivation, leadership in the workplace, and attitude investment. In July 2001, he launched his own publishing company, Dreams Unlimited Press (www.dreamsunlimitedpress.com). He is a member of the D.C. Chapter of the National Speakers Association and the Small Publishers Association of North America.

Peter lives in Germantown, Maryland, with his wife and business partner, Trevia-Lynne. He is currently working on his second book, *Invest in Your Attitude*.

If you'd like to book Peter for your next corporate or nonprofit event, or to find out more about his speaking topics and availability, please visit www.petercolwell.com or call (301) 515-6800.

About the Editor

Peter Vogt is President of Career Planning Resources in Minneapolis, and "The MonsterTRAK Coach" for MonsterTRAK.com, advising college students and recent graduates on their career-related concerns. Peter is also Producer of The Career Services Kiva, and his professional editing credits include 14 previously published books.

Visit www.careerplanningresources.com, www.monstertrak.com, and www.careerserviceskiva.com.

About the Designers

Tamara Dever and Erin Stark are co-proprietors of TLC Graphics, an award-winning book design firm with offices in Austin, TX and Waukesha, WI. Their company specializes in book cover design, interior layout, book promotions, and much more. Visit www.TLCGraphics.com.